A Special Bible

For

Geoffry Joe

From

Auntie & Uncle Victor Chung

Edmonton, Alberta

Hope You'll Make Good Use Of This.

Date

December 5, 1993

Christmas

"We will tell . . . about the praises of the Lord. We will tell about his power and the miracles he has done."
—Psalm 78:4

THE HOSANNA BIBLE

Stories retold by
Angela and Ken Abraham

Illustrations by
Terry Anderson and Kathleen Dunne

Concept by
Michael and Dorene Briggs

WORD PUBLISHING
Dallas·London·Vancouver·Melbourne

To Meaghan, Ashleigh, and Alyssa, and all their friends.
May the Lord's praises be ever on your lips and in your heart.

This book was written by Ken and Angela Abraham. Ken is the author of nineteen books. Angela is a freelance writer and a children's church coordinator for Christ Church in Nashville, Tennessee. The Abrahams have two daughters, Ashleigh and Alyssa.

Illustrations are by Terry Anderson and Kathleen Dunne through Rosenthal Represents, Los Angeles, California.

THE HOSANNA BIBLE

Text copyright © 1993 by Angela and Ken Abraham.
Art copyright © 1993 by Word Publishing.

Managing Editor: Laura Minchew   Project Editor: Beverly Phillips

Library of Congress Cataloging-in-Publication Data

Abraham, Angela, 1958–
    The Hosanna Bible / Angela and Ken Abraham ; Art by Rosenthal
Represents illustrations by Terry Anderson and Kathleen Dunne.
        p.   cm.
    "Word kids!"
    Summary : Simple retellings of more than 100 stories from the Old and
New Testaments.
    ISBN 0-8499-1036-6
    1. Bible stories, English. [1. Bible stories.] I. Abraham, Ken.
II. Anderson, Terry, ill. III. Dunne, Kathleen, 1933–   ill. IV. Title.
BS551.2.A33   1993
220.9'505—dc20   93–593
                                                                                        CIP
                                                                                        AC

Printed in the United States of America

3 4 5 6 7 8 9   RRD   9 8 7 6 5 4 3 2 1

Contents

OLD TESTAMENT

God's Garden	*(Genesis 1–2)*	1
The Fruit Tree	*(Genesis 3)*	5
Blood Brothers	*(Genesis 4)*	10
Rain, Rain, Go Away	*(Genesis 6–9:17)*	14
Chatter Scatter	*(Genesis 11:1–9)*	20
God's Promise	*(Genesis 12; 13; 15; 17; 18; 21:1–7)*	22
Jehovah–Jireh	*(Genesis 22:1–18)*	26
A Wife for Life	*(Genesis 24)*	30
The Twin That Wins	*(Genesis 25:19–34; 27:1–40)*	34
Bethel, "God's House"	*(Genesis 27:41–46; 28)*	38
A Fight at Night	*(Genesis 32–33:11)*	40
The Slave Who Forgave	*(Genesis 37; 39–50)*	44
Baby in a Basket	*(Exodus 1–2:10)*	54
A Special Stick	*(Exodus 2:11–4:13)*	58
Boils and Bugs	*(Exodus 4–11)*	61
The Chosen People	*(Exodus 11–13)*	66
Through the Sea	*(Exodus 14–15:21)*	68
Meat to Eat	*(Exodus 15:22–16)*	72
The Lord Is My Banner	*(Exodus 17:8–16)*	74
Holy Ground	*(Exodus 19–24)*	76
A Golden Calf	*(Exodus 32–33:6)*	80
God's Glory	*(Exodus 33–34)*	84
The Holy Tent	*(Exodus 31:1–11; 34:29; 35–36:8)*	87
The Traveling Church	*(Exodus 25–30; 37–40; Leviticus 1–9)*	90
Special Help	*(Numbers 11)*	94
Eye Spy	*(Numbers 13; 14; Deuteronomy 1:19–46)*	97
A Donkey That Talks	*(Numbers 22–24; 2 Peter 2:15–16)*	101
Be Strong! Be Brave!	*(Deuteronomy 31:1–8; Joshua 1; 3)*	106
Walls That Fall	*(Joshua 5:13–6)*	110
Stolen Treasure	*(Joshua 6:18–8:8)*	113
Two Women Save Israel	*(Judges 2:6–13; 4–5)*	116
God's Army	*(Judges 6–7)*	120
Samson's Secret	*(Judges 13; 14:5–6; 16:4–31)*	126
A Daughter's Love	*(Ruth)*	130
Hannah's Prayer	*(1 Samuel 1; 2:21)*	133

Samuel Hears a Voice   (1 Samuel 3)   135
Tall Saul   (1 Samuel 8–11)   139
The Singing Shepherd   (1 Samuel 15:10–23; 16)   142
Songs of Praise   (Psalms 8; 16; 33; 34)   146
Big Man, Little Man   (1 Samuel 17)   148
A Dance of Joy   (1 Samuel 18–19; 2 Samuel 5:1–5; 6–7;
                            1 Chronicles 15–17)   153
The Spirit Fills the Temple (1 Kings 2:1–4; 3:4–15; 5–9:9;
                            2 Chronicles 3–7)   157
Elijah the Prophet   (1 Kings 12–14; 16:29–17:16)   161
Victory on Mount Carmel   (1 Kings 18)   166
A Wind and a Whisper   (1 Kings 19)   170
The Battle Is the Lord's   (2 Chronicles 19–20:30)   174
The Chariot of Fire   (2 Kings 2:1–15)   179
A Dead Boy Sneezes   (2 Kings 4:8–37)   183
A Little Girl Helps   (2 Kings 5:1–16)   188
The Big Fish Near Tarshish (Jonah)   192
The King of Judah   (2 Kings 18–19; 2 Chronicles 32:1–23;
                            Isaiah 36–37)   197
Hezekiah's Healing   (2 Kings 20; 2 Chronicles 32:24; Isaiah 38)   201
The Boy King   (2 Kings 22–23:30)   203
A Prophet Who Cried   (Jeremiah 25; 29; 32; Lamentations 3:41–51)   207
The Fire Pit   (Daniel 1; 3)   210
A Secret Message   (Daniel 5)   214
Daniel in the Lions' Pit   (Daniel 6)   217
A Beauty Queen   (Esther)   221
Double Trouble   (Job)   225
Rebuilding the City   (Ezra 1–6; Nehemiah 1–6; 8–10;
                            Haggai 1:4, 8; Zechariah 4:6)   229

NEW TESTAMENT

An Angel Visits Mary   (Luke 1:26–56)   239
Zechariah's Prophecy   (Luke 1:5–25, 57–80)   244
God Became a Baby Boy   (Matthew 1:18–25; Luke 2:1–20)   248
Simeon Praises God   (Luke 2:21–38)   253
Wise Men Worship   (Matthew 2:1–12)   255
Lost and Found   (Luke 2:41–52)   257

Baptized!	*(Matthew 3:1–17; Mark 1:4–8;*	
	Luke 3:1–16; John 1:19–34)	260
The Dove from Above	*(Matthew 3:13–17; Mark 1:9–13;*	
	Luke 3:21–22; John 1:33–34)	263
Down with the Devil!	*(Matthew 4:1–11; Mark 1:12–13;*	
	Luke 4:1–13)	265
The First Miracle	*(John 2:1–11)*	268
Following Jesus	*(Luke 4:14–22; 5:1–11; 6:12–16;*	
	Matthew 4:18–22; Mark 1:16–20)	270
Healing the Sick	*(Mark 2:1–12; Luke 5:15–26)*	275
Preaching and Teaching	*(Matthew 5–7; Luke 6:20–49)*	279
Born Again	*(John 3:1–21)*	283
Jesus Puts Away the Demons	*(Mark 5:1–20; Luke 8:26–39)*	285
A Touch of Faith	*(Matthew 9:18–26; Mark 5:21–43;*	
	Luke 8:40–56)	288
Weeds and Seeds	*(Matthew 13:1–23; Mark 4:1–20;*	
	Luke 8:4–15)	293
Twelve Apostles Sent Out	*(Matthew 10:1–8, 20; Mark 6:7–13;*	
	Luke 9:1–6)	297
A Bunch for Lunch	*(Matthew 14:13–21; Mark 6:30–44;*	
	Luke 9:10–17; John 6:1–14)	300
Walking on Water	*(Matthew 14:22–33; Mark 6:45–52;*	
	John 6:16–21)	304
See His Glory	*(Matthew 17:1–13; Mark 9:2–13;*	
	Luke 9:28–36)	308
A Blind Man Sees	*(John 9)*	310
The Good Neighbor	*(Luke 10:25–37)*	314
The Lost Son	*(Luke 15:11–32)*	318
Lazarus Lives!	*(John 11:1–46)*	322
Jesus Blesses the Children	*(Matthew 18:1–14; 19:13–15;*	
	Mark 10:13–16; Luke 18:15–17)	327
Ten Healing Miracles	*(Luke 17:12–19)*	331
Mary Anoints Jesus	*(John 12:2–8)*	334
Hosanna to the King!	*(Matthew 21:1–9; Mark 11:1–10;*	
	Luke 19:29–40; John 12:12–19)	336
Jesus in the Temple	*(Matthew 21:12–17; Mark 11:15–18;*	
	Luke 19:45–48)	340
The Widow's Gift	*(Mark 12:41–44; Luke 21:1–4)*	343
The Master Serves His Followers	*(Matthew 26:17–19; Mark 14:12–14;*	
	Luke 22:7–13; John 13:1–20)	345

The Last Meal (Matthew 26:20–30; Mark 14:17–26; Luke 22:14–23; John 13:21–14:19; 16) 348

The Judas Kiss (Matthew 26:30–50; Mark 14:26–46; Luke 22:39–53; John 18:1–9) 353

Peter's Lie (Matthew 26:50–58, 69–75; Mark 14:46–54, 66–72; Luke 22:49–62; John 18:10–18, 25–27) 357

The Lamb of God (Matthew 26:59–68; 27:1–2, 11–31; Mark 14:55–65; 15:1–20; Luke 22:66–23:25; John 18:28–19:16) 360

The Cross (Matthew 27:26–60; Mark 15:17–46; Luke 23:26–53; John 19:16–42) 364

He's Alive! (Matthew 28:1–10; Mark 16:1–13; Luke 24:1–11) 368

A Mealtime Miracle (Mark 16:14–18; Luke 24:36–49; John 20:19–23; 1 Corinthians 15:5) 372

Jesus Goes Home (Mark 16:19–20; Luke 24:50–53; Acts 1:8–11) 376

Tongues of Fire (Acts 1:14; 2:1–21) 379

People of Power (Acts 2:14–47) 382

A Crippled Man Is Healed (Acts 3) 387

Can't Stop Talking (Acts 4:1–22) 389

Signs and Wonders (Acts 4:29–30; 5:12–42) 392

Stephen (Acts 6–7) 395

The Magician (Acts 8:2–25) 400

Philip Baptizes a Rich Man (Acts 8:26–40) 404

Saul Sees the Light (Acts 2:1–3; 9:1–19) 406

Paul in a Basket (Acts 9:20–25) 412

Rise and Be Healed! (Acts 9:36–43) 414

The Holy Spirit Is for Everyone (Acts 10) 416

A Mission (Acts 13:1–4) 420

Light and Darkness (Acts 13:6–12) 422

The Fortune–Teller (Acts 16:16–19) 424

Praises from Prison (Acts 16:19–34) 427

Paul Is Arrested (Acts 28:16–31) 431

Letters from Prison (1 Thessalonians 5:18–19; 2 Timothy 3:14–16; Ephesians 6:17–18; 1 Corinthians 16:13) 432

The City of God (Revelation 1:9–19; 4:2–11; 5:11–14; 7:16–17; 19:6; 21; 22:1–2, 5) 434

Christ's Return (Revelation 19:11–16; 22) 438

Old Testament

"**I** am the Lord your God. You must be holy
because I am holy."

—LEVITICUS 19:2

GOD'S GARDEN

Long ago, God made the world.
The earth was dark.
The sky was empty and black.
But God's Spirit looked over the world.
He had a wonderful plan!

When God spoke, the heavens appeared.
He blessed the earth with beauty.
God shaped the high mountains.
He filled the lakes with cool water.
He made the soft grass, fresh fruit, and bright
flowers that smell sweet.
God told the sun to shine in the day and the
stars to twinkle at night.

God made fish to splash and swim in the seas.
He made birds to sing and fly through
the air.
Then He filled the earth with animals:
Some that crawl and creep.
Some that jump and leap.
God said, "Let Us make someone to care for
My wonderful world!"

God molded a man from dirt and breathed
life into him.
He named the man Adam.
Then He formed a woman to help Adam.
Her name was Eve. God placed them in a
beautiful garden called Eden.
In six days, God made everything good.
On the seventh day, He rested from all His work.

THE FRUIT TREE

". . . In the middle of the garden, God put the tree that gives . . . the knowledge of good and evil." GENESIS *2:9*

Adam and Eve were happy in their special garden home. They walked and talked with God. He was their friend.

God told them, "You may eat fruit from any tree, except one. If you eat from the tree in the middle of the garden, you will die!"

Adam and Eve obeyed God.

One day, something terrible happened.
A sneaky snake asked Eve, "Did God really
tell you not to eat any of this tasty fruit?"
Eve looked at the beautiful fruit in the middle
of the garden.

"Taste some," said the snake. "It will make
you wise like God. You won't die."

Satan used the snake to trick Eve.
She ate the forbidden fruit.
Then she took some to Adam, and he tasted it.
Suddenly, Adam and Eve heard God walking
in the garden.
They had disobeyed God, so they were afraid.
Where could they hide from God?

"Adam, Adam, where are you?" God called.
"Why are you hiding?"
Adam answered, "I heard Your voice, and I
was frightened."
"Did you eat the fruit I told you not to
touch?" God asked.
"The woman gave it to me!" said Adam.
"The snake said it was okay to eat!" said Eve.

God was sad that they had not obeyed Him.
God cursed the snake. "You will crawl on
your belly forever!"
God told Adam and Eve, "Because you chose
to sin, you must leave the garden."
Then He made animal clothing for them to
wear and sent them away from their lovely
garden home.

BLOOD BROTHERS

"If you do good, I will accept you. But if you do not do good, sin is ready to attack you. Sin wants you. But you must rule over it." GENESIS *4:7*

Adam and Eve had many children.
Their first sons were named Cain and Abel.
Cain was a farmer.
Abel took care of sheep.

One day Cain and Abel were worshiping
God. They each brought God a gift.
Abel's gift was good.
But Cain's gift was selfish.
Cain's gift did not please God.

Cain was angry that God did not accept his offering. Cain wanted to kill Abel.
"Your heart is angry," God said. "Do good and I will accept you." But Cain did not obey God.
Cain hit Abel and killed him.

"Where is your brother?" God asked.
Cain yelled, "I don't know. Is it my job to
take care of him?"
God said, "I see what you did to your brother.
You will be punished for the terrible way
you treated him."
God told Cain, "Your heart is evil. You
cannot stay in My presence."
Cain roamed the earth without God.

RAIN, RAIN, GO AWAY

"The Lord said, 'My Spirit will not remain in human beings forever. . . .'"
GENESIS 6:3

The earth was crowded with wicked people.
God was sorry that He made man.
He said, "I will destroy everything on earth
and start again!"
But God saw one good man who tried to
do right.

14

God told Noah, "I will drown the earth in a
flood of water. You will be saved, if you
build a big boat."
Noah did everything God said.
He built a boat tall and wide.
His family and many animals would hide
safely inside.

Noah put two of every kind of animal on the boat—alligators, elephants, monkeys, and bears; every animal pair marched onto the boat. And God shut the door tight.

Thunder and lightning crashed.
Rain poured from the sky.
It stormed for forty days and nights.
The water rose high above the mountain peaks.

Finally, God sent a wind to dry the earth.
And the boat touched solid ground.
Then Noah sent a dove from the boat.
The dove returned with an olive leaf in his
beak. And Noah knew that the ground was
almost dry.

When Noah left the boat, he built an altar.
He thanked God for saving his family.
God was very pleased. He blessed Noah.
God said, "I will never again destroy the
earth with a flood. A rainbow in the sky will
be the sign of My promise to you."

CHATTER SCATTER

"Then they said to each other, 'Let's build for ourselves a city and a tower. And let's make the top of the tower reach high into the sky. We will become famous. . . .'" GENESIS 11:4

Soon the earth was full of people again. Everyone used the same language to talk. The people said, "Let's build a city with a tall tower to show how wonderful we are." These proud people thought they were greater than God.

God was not happy. So he mixed up their speech. The people stopped building the tower and scattered to every land.
And the city was named *Babel*, which means "confusion." From then on, people living in different lands spoke their own languages.

GOD'S PROMISE

". . . The Lord said, 'I am God All-Powerful. Obey me and do what is right. I will make an agreement between us. I will make you the ancestor of many people.'" GENESIS *17:1, 2*

Abram worshiped God.
His neighbors prayed to false gods.
God told Abram, "Leave this country.
Go to a new land, and I will bless you."
Abram obeyed God.

Abram packed all his things and moved.
Then God appeared to Abram,
"I will give to your family all the land you see."
Abram thanked God.

One night God spoke to Abram in a vision,
"Can you count the stars at night?
I will bless you with so many children,
you will not be able to count them."
Later God changed Abram's name to Abraham.
Again, God said, "You will be father of many."

Abraham was now ninety-nine years old.
God said, "Your wife, Sarah, will have a son."
Abraham said, "Sarah and I are too old to have children."
"Is anything too hard for the Lord?" said God.
Isaac was the son born to Sarah and Abraham.
Isaac means "laughter."

JEHOVAH-JIREH

"So Abraham named that place The Lord Gives. Even today people say, 'On the mountain of the Lord it will be given.'" GENESIS 22:14

One day God tested Abraham's love.
He said, "Abraham, I want you to give up
your only son." He told Abraham to sacrifice
Isaac on an altar.
This was a terribly hard thing to do.
Abraham loved Isaac very much.
But Abraham also trusted God.

Early the next morning, Abraham took Isaac
to a mountain and built an altar.
Isaac said, "Father, where is the lamb for the
sacrifice?"
Abraham said, "God will take care of it."

Then Abraham laid his son on the altar.
Suddenly, the angel of God shouted,
"Abraham! Abraham! Do not hurt the boy.
Since you have obeyed Me, I now know that
you love God most."

Then Abraham saw a ram caught by his horns in the bushes. Abraham sacrificed the ram instead of his only son.

Abraham named that place *Jehovah-Jireh,* which means, "The Lord will provide." God blessed Abraham with a great reward because he trusted the Lord.

A WIFE FOR LIFE

". . . 'The Lord will send his angel before you. The angel will help you get a wife for my son there.'" GENESIS *24:7*

It was time for Isaac to find a wife.
The local girls worshiped false gods.
Abraham worried. His grandchildren might
become idol worshipers if Isaac married a
local girl.

Abraham said to his loyal servant, "Go to my homeland and bring back a wife for Isaac." "How will I choose the girl?" the servant asked. "The Lord will send His angel before you. He will help you," said Abraham.

The servant traveled to Abraham's old town.
He stopped by a well to pray,
"Lord, please lead me to the right girl."
The young girls from town were walking
toward the well. The servant prayed, "When
I ask for a drink, let the girl for Isaac
answer me."

Just then, a beautiful girl named Rebekah
came to the well. She gave the servant a
drink of water. She said, "I will get your
camels a drink, too."

The servant praised God for answering his
prayer. "God has been kind and truthful.
Rebekah is the right wife for Isaac's life."

THE TWIN THAT WINS

"Esau said, 'Jacob is the right name for him. He has tricked me these two times. He took away my share of everything you own. And now he has taken away my blessing.'" GENESIS *27:36*

After Abraham died, his son Isaac became the owner of all his tents, sheep, cattle, camels, and servants.
Now, Isaac and Rebekah had twin boys.
Esau was the oldest son.
He would receive more of his father's riches and God's promises.
Jacob was the younger brother.

One day, Esau came in from hunting.
Jacob was cooking some vegetable soup.
"Mmm, that soup smells good. I'm starved.
Let me have a bite!" said Esau.
"Sure, if you sell me your part of father's
wealth," said Jacob slyly.
Esau did not appreciate the promises of God.
He sold his future riches for a bowl of soup.

When Isaac was old and blind,
he called for Esau, "I want to give you God's
blessing before I die. Go hunting for an
animal that is good to eat. Then make me a
tasty meal. I will bless you after dinner."
Rebekah heard Isaac's words. She told Jacob
how to get the blessing Isaac was going to
give Esau.

Isaac could not see, so Jacob pretended to be
Esau. Jacob dressed like his brother and raced
to Isaac's tent.

"Is that really you, Esau? Come closer so I can
touch you," said Isaac. Jacob wore animal
skins to make his skin feel hairy like Esau's.
Jacob tricked Isaac into giving him the
blessing.

BETHEL, "GOD'S HOUSE"

"Then Jacob woke from his sleep. He said, 'Surely the Lord is in this place.'" GENESIS 28:16

Esau hated Jacob for stealing his blessing.
Rebekah warned Jacob, "You must leave this
place before Esau tries to kill you. Go to your
grandfather's old home and hide."
Jacob started his long journey.
One night, he used a stone for a pillow.
In a dream he saw angels climbing up and
down a ladder to heaven.
God was standing above the ladder. He said,
"I will give you the land where you are
sleeping. And I will protect you everywhere
you go."

When Jacob woke up he said, "Surely the Lord is in this place." He named the place *Bethel*, which means "house of God."

A FIGHT AT NIGHT

"So Jacob named that place Peniel. He said, 'I have seen God face to face. But my life was saved.'" GENESIS *32:30*

Many years passed before Jacob went back home.
God had blessed him with great wealth.
He was married and had many children.
One day, he got news that Esau was nearby.
Esau had an army of men.
Jacob feared for his family's safety.

Jacob prayed, "Lord, You said You would watch over me! I am afraid Esau will kill us! Please, protect us."

Jacob prepared a very special gift of many animals for Esau.

Jacob thought, *"Esau might forgive me when he sees this gift."*

That night, Jacob prayed again.
A man wrestled with him until morning.
Jacob's leg was hurt, but he would not stop
struggling.
"You can't go until you bless me," said Jacob.
The man said, "Your name will be changed
from Jacob to Israel. For you have wrestled
with God and won the victory!"

Later, Jacob saw Esau.
Jacob bowed low before him.
Esau had forgiven his brother.
He ran to Jacob and kissed him.
The brothers cried. They were happy to see
each other.

THE SLAVE WHO FORGAVE

"Then Joseph said to them, 'Don't be afraid. . . . You meant to hurt me. But God turned your evil into good. . . . I will take care of you and your children. . . .'" GENESIS 50:19–21

Jacob lived in the land of Canaan with his
twelve sons. Joseph was his favorite son.
Jacob made Joseph a colorful coat.
All the brothers were jealous.
When Joseph had a strange dream, his
brothers hated him even more.

"Brothers, listen to my dream," Joseph said
proudly. "We were in the field tying bundles
of wheat. My bundle of wheat stood up. Your
bundles bowed down to mine."

"Do you want to be our king?" Joseph's
brothers asked angrily.

Before long, Joseph dreamed again that his
family would bow down to him.

One day, Joseph's brothers grabbed him.
They tore off his bright coat and threw him
in a pit. Then a group of traders passed by.
"Let's sell Joseph to the traders," the brothers
agreed. They sold him for twenty pieces of
silver.
The traders took Joseph to Egypt and sold
him as a slave.

Joseph worked hard in Egypt.
God blessed everything he did.
Soon, his master put him in charge of all the
master owned. Then the master's wife lied
about Joseph.
Joseph was thrown into prison, even though
he was not guilty. But God was with Joseph
there.

One night, the king of Egypt had two
dreams. No one in Egypt could explain the
meaning to him. Someone told the king that
Joseph could explain dreams. The king sent
for Joseph.

When Joseph heard the dreams, he told the
king that God was warning him.

"There will be seven years of plenty in Egypt,
followed by seven years of hunger," Joseph
said.

"We should store up food during the years of plenty. Then everyone will have enough food during the famine."

The king said, "Joseph, you are filled with the spirit of God, and you are wise. I want you to be in charge of the food project."

The king gave Joseph the highest position in the land, next to the king.

Everything that Joseph said would happen
came true. Egypt was the only land that
saved food for the famine years. Hungry
people came from every country to Egypt.
One day, Joseph's brothers came all the way
from Canaan to buy food.

They did not know they would have to buy
their food from Joseph.
All the brothers bowed down before the
governor of Egypt.
They did not know he was Joseph.

Joseph recognized his brothers. But he kept quiet until they visited again.

"Brothers, it is I, Joseph," he finally said. "Don't be afraid of me. God turned into good what you meant to be evil."

Joseph told his brothers to move to Egypt so they would have plenty to eat.

Jacob was happy when he heard that Joseph was alive. He built an altar to thank God.

At last Jacob's family reached Egypt. Joseph came in his chariot to meet them. He couldn't wait to see his father.

BABY IN A BASKET

"'I am . . . the God of your father. Don't be afraid to go to Egypt.
I will make your descendants a great nation there. . . . And I
will bring you out of Egypt again.'" GENESIS *46:3, 4*

At first, the children of Jacob were treated
well in Egypt. The family grew larger, and
they were called Israelites.
Many years passed.
There was a new king in Egypt.
He did not know Joseph or the wonderful
way he had saved the hungry people.

He feared the Israelites would soon out-
number his own people.
So, he made them his slaves.
He made them work hard.
Still, the children of Israel grew in numbers.
To stop this, the evil king decided to kill all of
the Israelite baby boys.

A mother hid her baby in a basket by the river. One day, the king's daughter came to the river to bathe. She found the baby in the basket. The baby started to cry, and she felt sorry for him. She adopted the baby as her own son and named him Moses.

Moses grew up as a prince in the palace.
Meanwhile, God's people suffered as slaves.
One day, Moses saw an Egyptian man
beating an Israelite slave.
Moses killed the Egyptian.
When the king found out, he wanted to kill
Moses. But Moses ran away to hide in the
desert.

A SPECIAL STICK

"Then God said to Moses, 'I AM WHO I AM.' When you go to the people of Israel, tell them, 'I AM has sent me to you.'" EXODUS 3:14

One day, Moses saw a burning bush that did not burn up.

God called to Moses from the bush, "Moses! Moses! Take off your shoes. Do not come any closer to Me. You are standing on holy ground."

Moses covered his face. He was afraid.

The Lord said, "I have heard the prayers of My people. Go tell the king to free My people so they can worship Me. I want you to lead My people out of Egypt."

Moses said, "I'm not a great man. What if the people of Israel do not want me for their leader?"

God said, "Tell them *Yahweh* sent you. I AM WHO I AM."

The Lord told Moses to throw down his
walking stick. Moses did. And the stick
changed into a hissing snake.
God said, "Grab the snake by its tail."
Moses was afraid, but he obeyed God. The
snake turned back into a stick.
God said, "Show My people this miracle.
They will know *Yahweh* has sent you."

BOILS AND BUGS

"Moses said to the Lord, 'But Lord, I am not a skilled speaker. . . .'
Then the Lord said to him, 'Who made man's mouth? . . . Now
go! I will tell you what to say.'" EXODUS 4:10, 11, 12

Moses told God, "I'm not a good speaker."
God said, "Your brother Aaron will speak
for you."
Aaron and Moses went to see the king of
Egypt. They said, "God wants you to let His
people go!"
The king said angrily, "I don't know your God."
The mean king made the Israelite slaves work
even harder.

Moses was discouraged.

God told him, "I am the Lord, God All-Powerful.

Now you will see what I will do to the king."

God turned all the water in Egypt to blood.

The Egyptians had no water to drink.

The Israelites' water stayed pure.

But the king would not let God's people go.

Aaron raised the special stick over all the waters of Egypt, and the land was filled with frogs. The king said to Moses, "Ask your God to take the frogs away. I will let your people go." Then Moses prayed, and God removed the frogs. But the king broke his promise. He would not let God's people go.

God punished Egypt with terrible plagues.
He covered their land with bugs. He caused
their animals to die. Both people and
animals got horrible sores. The crops were
killed in a hail storm. Then locusts ate all the
plants the storm didn't kill.
Finally, it was dark in Egypt for three days.
Still, the stubborn king refused to listen to God.

Moses went to see the king one last time.
Moses said, "Tonight, every firstborn son in
Egypt will die. But the Israelites will be
unharmed."
The king did not listen. He yelled, "Get out
of here, or I will kill you!"

THE CHOSEN PEOPLE

"When I see the blood, I will pass over you. . . . You are always to remember this day. Celebrate it with a feast to the Lord. . . ."
EXODUS *12:13, 14*

The Lord told the Israelites what to do to get ready for "the Passover."
Each family cooked a lamb for a special meal. They wiped the lamb's blood on the sides and top of their door frames.
That night, every firstborn son of the Egyptians died. But God protected the Israelites. He passed over every home that had blood on the door frame.

During the night, the king called for Moses.
He said, "Take your people out of this land.
Go worship your God."
The Egyptian people gave their jewelry and
riches to the Israelites.
The Egyptians were afraid of Israel's God.
All the Israelites quickly packed and left
Egypt together.

THROUGH THE SEA

" ' I will sing to the Lord because he is worthy of great honor. He has thrown the horse and its rider into the sea. The Lord gives me strength and makes me sing. He has saved me. He is my God, and I will praise him.' " EXODUS 15:1, 3

God led the people of Israel out of Egypt. During the day, He traveled ahead of the Israelites in a great cloud.

At night, He was a pillar of fire, so they were not in darkness. The Lord God showed His children which way to go.

The Israelites followed the Lord's great cloud to the edge of the Red Sea.

When the king of Egypt realized he had let all his slaves go, he changed his mind.

He chased after the Israelites with his army.

The Israelites were terrified when they saw the king's chariots racing after them.

Moses said, "Don't be afraid! Stand still and watch the Lord fight for you!"

The Lord caused the water to separate. The Israelites crossed the sea on dry land.

The king's chariots chased after the children of Israel.

When the Israelites got to the other side, the water came back together. And the king's army drowned in the sea.

Then, Moses and the Israelites sang praises to the Lord. Moses' sister, Miriam, took a tambourine in her hand. All the women followed her, playing tambourines and dancing.

MEAT TO EAT

" ' You must obey the Lord, your God . . . and keep his rules. If you do these things, I will not give you any of the sicknesses I gave the Egyptians.' " EXODUS 15:26

The Israelites traveled through the desert for three days. They started complaining to Moses because they had no water. Then the water they found was bitter, so the Lord showed Moses a tree to put in the water to make it taste good.

God said, "You must obey Me. If you do, I will keep you well. I am the Lord who heals you."

Soon, the people began grumbling to Moses
again. "We don't have any meat to eat,"
they said.

"In Egypt we had plenty of food. Are we
going to starve in the desert?"

The Lord sent them quail and manna from
heaven. The people had bread and meat to
eat each day.

THE LORD IS MY BANNER

"Then Moses built an altar. He named it THE LORD IS MY BANNER. Moses said, 'I lifted my hands toward the Lord's throne.'"
EXODUS 17:15, 16

The Israelites stopped to rest in the desert. Suddenly, wild people who lived in the hills attacked them. Moses quickly called out all the men who were prepared to fight.
He made Joshua their leader.
The Israelites went to war against the wild people. Moses raised his hands toward heaven. He prayed for God to help His people.

When Moses' hands were lifted up, the Israelites won. When Moses got tired, he let his arms drop down. And the enemy started to win. Two men stood beside Moses. They held his hands high until God's children won the battle. Then Moses called the place *Jehovah-Nissi* which means, "The Lord Is My Banner."

HOLY GROUND

" 'You must worship the Lord your God. If you do, I will bless your bread and your water. I will take away sickness from you. . . . I will allow you to live long lives.' " EXODUS 23:25, 26

Finally, the Israelites reached the Sinai Mountain. This was the place where God had spoken to Moses from the burning bush. The Lord called Moses to the mountain. He said, "Tell the people they must wash their clothes. They must prepare themselves for service to God. Then, I will come down on the mountain."

The Lord warned Moses, "Do not let the people touch the mountain. This is a holy place where I will show My glory."
Three days later, the people heard a loud trumpet blast and thunder. They saw fire and lightning. A thick cloud covered the mountain. The people were frightened. They heard the voice of God speak to Moses.

God called Moses to the mountain top.
God said, "I am the Lord your God.
I brought you out of slavery in Egypt."
Then God gave ten rules to help His people
live right. He wrote them on stone tablets.

*I am the only, one true God. Love and
    worship Me.*
Do not worship or serve any other god.
Do not curse or swear using God's name.
Rest on the Sabbath day; keep it holy.
Honor your father and mother.
Do not kill people.
Husbands and wives be faithful to each other.
Do not steal.
Do not lie.
*Do not wish for things that belong to someone
    else.*

God told Moses, "I've written My rules.
Now you can teach them to the people."

A GOLDEN CALF

"And the Lord said to Moses, '. . . They have quickly turned away from the things I commanded them to do.'" EXODUS *32:7–8*

Moses stayed on the mountain forty days. The people thought he wasn't coming back. They no longer feared the Lord's presence nor kept His rules.

One day the people said to Aaron, "Make us
a god we can see."
He melted their gold jewelry and molded it
into the shape of a calf.
The people bowed down to worship it.

The Lord told Moses, "Hurry down the
mountain. The people are worshiping
another god. They have made Me angry.
Now, I will destroy them!"

"Lord, please forget Your anger," Moses
begged. "Remember Your promises to us."
The Lord listened to Moses and did not
destroy the Israelites.

Moses returned to the Israelite camp.
He found the wicked people dancing around
the golden calf. Moses smashed the stone
tablets on the ground. Then, he set fire to the
golden calf. He ground the melted gold into
powder. Then he threw it into the water and
forced the people to drink it.

GOD'S GLORY

"Then Moses said, 'Now, please show me your greatness.' The Lord answered, 'I will cause all my goodness to pass in front of you. . . . But you cannot see my face . . . and stay alive.'" Exodus *33:18-20*

The Lord told Moses, "Prepare two stone tablets. Bring them to Me on the mountain. I will write down My rules once more." Moses stayed forty more days on the mountain with God. The Lord God in all His glory passed by Moses.
But Moses did not see God's face.

The Lord said, "I am a kind and loving God. I do not get angry quickly. I forgive My people for their sins. But, I remember to punish the wicked."

Moses bowed to the ground and worshiped God.

"Lord, please forgive these stubborn, sinful people," Moses prayed.

The Lord said, "All right. I will make an agreement with you. I will do miracles that have never been seen before. The people will see My power. And you must obey My rules."

THE HOLY TENT

"Then Moses said to the people of Israel, . . . 'The Lord has given Bezalel the skill, ability and knowledge to do all kinds of work . . . to build the Holy Tent.'" EXODUS *35:30, 31; 36:1*

When Moses returned to camp, his face glowed like the sun. God had given Moses the plans for building a Holy Tent. Now, the people would have a place to worship God.

Moses said to the people, "Everyone who
wants to give may bring a gift to God.
This will help us to build the Holy Tent."
The people brought jewelry of silver and
gold. They brought colorful cloth and special
wood. They gave more than what was
needed to build the house of God!

Then God filled a man named Bezalel with His Spirit. He gave him and others special skills to build the Holy Tent.

THE TRAVELING CHURCH

"Then the cloud covered the Meeting Tent. The greatness of the Lord filled the Holy Tent. . . . When the cloud rose from the Holy Tent, the Israelites would begin to travel." EXODUS 40:34, 36

When the tent was completed, Moses held a special service. He sprinkled oil on the Holy Box with God's laws in it. Moses anointed everything in the tent with oil to make it holy.

Moses washed Aaron and his sons with water.
Then Moses poured the anointing oil on
them, to prepare them for service to God.
The Lord had chosen them to be His priests.
After seven days, Aaron offered sacrifices for
the sins of the people.

Aaron lifted up his hands and blessed the
people. Then, the Lord's glory came to all the
people.

Holy fire came upon the altar and burned up
the sacrifices. When the people saw this, they
shouted for joy. Then they bowed down to
worship the Lord.

Since the Israelites moved from place to place, the Holy Tent was like a "traveling church." It stood in the middle of camp for everyone to see. God's great cloud covered it all through the day. At night, the Lord showed His presence in a blaze of fire above His tent. Whenever God's great cloud or holy fire moved, the Israelites followed it.

SPECIAL HELP

*"The Lord said to Moses, 'Bring me 70 of Israel's older leaders. . . .
I will take some of the Spirit that is in you. And I will give it to them.
They will help you care for the people.'"* NUMBERS *11:16, 17*

The Israelites started complaining about all
their troubles in the desert. They forgot to be
thankful for God's daily miracles.
The Lord became angry. His fire burned up
part of the camp. The people cried out to
Moses for help.
When Moses prayed, the fire stopped.

The Lord told Moses to bring seventy of
Israel's leaders to the Holy Tent and He
would give him some help.
The Lord spoke through the great cloud.
Then, the Holy Spirit came upon them all,
and they prophesied. Moses was glad to have
help.

Next, the Lord taught the grumblers a lesson.
They had complained about having no
meat. So God sent them quail to eat. They
had to eat it every day for a month. And they
hated it. It made them terribly sick.

EYE SPY

" 'The land we went to explore is very good. . . . Don't be afraid of the people in that land! . . . They have no protection, but we have the Lord.' " NUMBERS 14:7, 9

One day the Israelites camped close to Canaan. This was the land God had promised them.

Moses sent twelve men to scout out the land. "Look at the land. Notice where the cities are. See how strong the enemy is. Then, bring back your report," Moses told them.

The twelve spies scouted the land for forty days.
They returned to camp with samples of fruit.
The people were excited to see the huge
grape clusters and fresh figs.
The men said, "The land is beautiful, with
plenty of fruit and water. But . . . the people
who live there are like giants."

"We felt like grasshoppers beside them," said
ten of the spies. "They are too strong for us."
But two spies, Caleb and Joshua, said, "Don't
be afraid of the people in the land. The Lord
is on our side. He will lead us into the land."
But the Israelites believed what the ten spies
said and started grumbling again.

The Lord said to Moses, "How long will it be before these people believe Me?"
The Lord was very angry.
He made the Israelites wander in the wilderness for forty more years. Only Joshua, Caleb, and the younger generations were allowed to enter into the Promised Land.

A DONKEY THAT TALKS

"Then the Spirit of God entered him. And Balaam gave this message: . . . 'Anyone who blesses you will be blessed. And anyone who curses you will be cursed.'" NUMBERS *24:2, 3, 9*

Now, the surrounding countries feared Israel. King Balak was terrified to see them marching near his land. Balak wanted to drive Israel back into the desert. He sent a message to Balaam, the prophet: "Come and curse these Israelites. I will give you a great reward."

But God warned Balaam. "Do not curse Israel,"
He said. "I have already blessed them."
God told Balaam, "Go to Balak. But only do
what I tell you." Balaam saddled his donkey
and traveled toward Balak's country.

God knew Balaam really wanted the reward from Balak. God sent an angel with a sword to stop Balaam. Balaam's donkey saw the angel but Balaam didn't.

The donkey ran off the road. Balaam hit him and forced him back onto the road.

The Lord made Balaam's donkey talk. "Why are you hitting me?"

Balaam said, "You're making me look like a fool!"

"Have I ever done this before?" said the donkey.

Suddenly, Balaam saw the angel and
fell to the ground. "I have sinned," said
Balaam. "I did not see you blocking the
road." So Balaam blessed Israel instead of
cursing them.

BE STRONG! BE BRAVE!

"So the Lord said to Moses, 'Take Joshua son of Nun. My Spirit is in him. Put your hand on him. . . . Let him share your honor. Then all the Israelites will obey him.'" NUMBERS 27:18, 20

After Moses died, Joshua became the Israelites' leader. The Lord told Joshua to cross the Jordan River and lead the people into the Promised Land.

The Lord said, "Joshua, be strong and brave! Don't be afraid. I will be with you everywhere you go."

Joshua told the people, "Get ready. In three days, we will cross the Jordan River."

The people answered, "Anything you tell us
to do, we will obey."
They traveled to the Jordan River and
camped there before crossing it. Joshua said,
"Tomorrow, God will do amazing things."
The Israelites prayed.
They believed God would perform a miracle
for them to enter the Promised Land.

The next day, Joshua told the priests to go to the river and step into the water. The priests obeyed Joshua. They carried the Holy Box from the Holy Tent to show that God was with them. At the moment they stepped into the river, the water stopped flowing.

The priests walked to the middle of the river
and waited. All the people of Israel crossed
the Jordan River on dry ground.
Then the priests carried the Holy Box to the
other side. As soon as their feet touched the
riverbank, the water became deep again.

WALLS THAT FALL

"The Lord spoke to Joshua. He said, 'Look, I have given you Jericho. . . . The walls of the city will fall.'" Joshua 6:2, 5

Joshua was near the city of Jericho.
Suddenly, a man with a sword appeared.
"I am the Commander of the Lord's army,"
he said. "Take off your sandals. You are
standing on holy ground."
Joshua realized it was the Lord. So Joshua
removed his shoes and bowed down.

The Lord told Joshua how to capture the city
in seven days.
Following God's plan, the priests led the
Israelite army around Jericho. Once a day,
the soldiers silently circled the city.

On the seventh day, they marched around
Jericho seven times. Then the priests blew
their trumpets.

Joshua cried out, "Shout, for the Lord has
given you the city!"

When everyone shouted, the strong walls
shook and fell down. Israel won the battle.

STOLEN TREASURE

"'The Lord, the God of Israel, says some of you are keeping things he commanded you to destroy. You will never defeat your enemies until you throw away those things.'" JOSHUA 7:13

There was great treasure in Jericho. So Joshua said it must be given to the Lord.
Everything else was to be destroyed.
But a man named Achan disobeyed. He found a beautiful coat and some shiny gold and silver. He took the treasure to his tent and hid it. Achan robbed God!

Later, Joshua sent a small army to attack the tiny town of Ai. But Ai defeated them. And the Israelites were afraid.

Joshua prayed, "Lord, why did You let this happen to us?"

The Lord told Joshua, "Israel has stolen from Me. I will not help you defeat your enemies unless you obey Me."

God showed Joshua that Achan was the robber.
The treasure was found in Achan's tent.
And he was stoned to death for stealing.
Afterwards, Joshua sent another army against Ai. This time, Israel won the battle easily.

TWO WOMEN SAVE ISRAEL

"On that day Deborah and Barak son of Abinoam sang this song: 'The leaders led Israel. The people volunteered to go to battle. Praise the Lord! I myself will sing to the Lord. I will make music to the LORD, the God of Israel.'" JUDGES 5:1-3

After Joshua died, the Israelites forgot their promises to serve the Lord God.
They prayed to gods of wood and stone.
Israel became weak without God's strength.
An evil general, named Sisera, attacked Israel with his mighty army.
Finally the Israelites begged God for help.

At that time, Deborah was a leader in Israel. God's Spirit was upon her, and she was very wise. Deborah told the people what God wanted to say to them.

She told a man named Barak, "Call out the men to fight. The Lord will help you defeat Sisera."

But Barak was afraid.

Deborah said, "Since you don't trust God for the victory, a woman will win this war." When they went to battle, Israel's army surprised the enemy.
Sisera's army ran away.
Sisera ran to a tent that belonged to a woman named Jael.
"Come in, General Sisera," Jael said. "You may hide here."

General Sisera was thirsty and tired from running. Jael gave him a jug of milk, and he slept soundly.

While Sisera was sleeping, Jael killed the evil general. Then she showed Barak what she had done.

The women Deborah and Jael won the victory for Israel because they trusted the Lord.

GOD'S ARMY

"Then Gideon said to the Lord, 'If you are pleased with me, give me proof. Show me that it is really you talking with me.'" Judges 6:17

For seven years, the Midianites attacked Israel. Then the angel of the Lord appeared to Gideon and said, "I have given you the strength to save Israel."

Gideon said, "Lord, why me? I am poor and
unimportant. What can I do?"
The Lord said, "I will be with you."
But, Gideon was unsure.

One night, Gideon asked God for proof.
He said, "I will put some wool outside.
Tomorrow, if the wool is wet and the ground
is dry, I will know that You are with me."

The next morning, the wool was full of water
and the ground was dry.
Gideon still doubted God. He said,
"Tomorrow let the ground be wet and the
wool be dry."
And that is exactly what God did.

The Spirit of God entered Gideon. After that, thousands of men stepped forward to follow him. The Lord said to Gideon, "Your army is too large. Tell the men who are afraid that they may go home."

Finally, Gideon chose 300 men to be in his army. God told him to give each man a trumpet and a jar with a burning torch inside.

That night, Gideon's small army surrounded
the enemy camp. All at once, Gideon and
his men blew their trumpets and smashed
their jars.

They shouted, "A sword for the Lord and for
Gideon!"

The scared Midianite army ran away.

SAMSON'S SECRET

"The angel of the Lord appeared to Manoah's wife. He said, 'You have not been able to have children. But you will become pregnant and have a son! . . . You must never cut his hair because he will be a Nazirite. He will be given to God from birth.'" JUDGES 13:3, 5

One day the angel of the Lord surprised Manoah and his wife.
"Soon you will have a son," he said.
"You must never cut his hair. This will be a sign that he belongs to God. Your son will help rescue Israel from her enemies."
Manoah and his wife named their baby Samson.

When Samson grew up, the Spirit of the Lord gave him great power. He became the strongest man that ever lived. One afternoon Samson killed a lion with his bare hands. Then he used his great strength to fight against God's enemies. For many years, Samson was a leader in Israel.

Samson loved a woman named Delilah.
Enemies paid Delilah to find out the secret of
Samson's strength. Delilah tricked Samson,
and he said, "My hair has never been cut."
While he was sleeping, Delilah called a man
to cut Samson's hair. When Samson woke up,
his strength was gone.

The enemy made Samson blind and put him
in prison.

One day Samson's enemies brought him to a
big party in honor of their false gods. They
wanted to make fun of him. Samson prayed,
"Lord, give me strength again!"
Samson pushed on the pillars that held up
the ceiling. And the building crashed down
on the evil people. The Lord had helped
Samson defeat the enemy one last time.

A DAUGHTER'S LOVE

"But Ruth said, 'Don't ask me to leave you! Don't beg me not to follow you! Every place you go, I will go. Every place you live, I will live. Your people will be my people. Your God will be my God.'" Ruth 1:16

Naomi lived in the country of Moab. It was far away from her hometown of Bethlehem. Naomi was sad because her husband and sons had died. She decided to move back to Bethlehem. Naomi told her daughter-in-law Ruth, "I am old and poor. You are young and beautiful. Stay here in your own country and remarry."

Naomi was a good woman, and Ruth loved
her dearly. Ruth said, "I will stay with you. I
will go wherever you go. Your people will be
my people. Your God will be my God." So
Ruth left her friends and family to travel with
Naomi to the city of Bethlehem.
The two widows were very poor.

Ruth gathered grain in a nearby field, so
they would have food to eat. A rich man
named Boaz owned the land.
He noticed Ruth working hard in his field.
Boaz saw that Ruth was kind to her mother-
in-law. Boaz married Ruth, and they had a
baby boy. Now Naomi and Ruth were happy
because God had given them a new family.

HANNAH'S PRAYER

"'I prayed for this child. The Lord answered my prayer and gave him to me. . . . He will belong to the Lord all his life. . . .'" 1 SAMUEL 1:27, 28

Hannah wanted a baby very much.
She prayed to God for a son. She promised he would do God's work all his life.
Eli, the priest, saw Hannah praying. "Go in peace," he said. "May God answer your prayer."
And the Lord God blessed Hannah with a baby boy. She named him Samuel, which means "Asked of God."

Hannah remembered her promise to God.
When Samuel was still a small child, she
took him to Eli at the Holy Tent.
And Samuel lived with the priest.
God was good to Hannah because she kept
her promise. Hannah became the mother of
three sons and two daughters.

SAMUEL HEARS A VOICE

"Samuel said, 'Speak, Lord. I am your servant, and I am listening.'"
1 SAMUEL 3:10

One night, little Samuel was sleeping in the
Holy Tent. A voice called his name.
Samuel ran to Eli and said, "Here I am.
What do you want me to do?"
Eli said, "I didn't call you. Go back to bed."

Samuel went back to bed. Soon, he heard the voice calling him again. Samuel rushed to Eli's side. "I am here. You called me," he said.

"No, I didn't," Eli said. "Go lie down."
Eli realized the Lord was calling Samuel.
Eli said, "When you hear the voice again,
say, 'Speak, Lord. I am listening.'"

So, the Lord spoke to Samuel.
From then on, Samuel gave God's messages
to the people. And all the messages came
true. Samuel was a prophet and ruler in
Israel for many years.

TALL SAUL

"'You must honor the Lord and serve him. You must obey his commands. Both you and the king ruling over you must follow the Lord your God. If you do, it will be well with you.'" 1 SAMUEL *12:14*

When Samuel was old, the people asked him to choose a king to lead them. They said, "All the other countries have kings. We want a king, too."

Samuel was not pleased.

"Do what the people ask," the Lord told him. "But warn them a king will bring trouble."

At this time, there lived a young man named
Saul. Several of his father's donkeys had
wandered away, and Saul was searching for
them. Saul went to see Samuel, the prophet.
He hoped the wise man would help him find
the donkeys. When Samuel saw the tall,
young Saul, the Lord said, "Anoint this man
ruler over My people."

Samuel poured oil over Saul's head and
anointed him the first king of Israel. Then
the Spirit of the Lord entered Saul, and he
prophesied. Saul was a good king, as long as
he listened to Samuel and obeyed God.

THE SINGING SHEPHERD

"'God does not see the same way people see. People look at the outside of a person, but the Lord looks at the heart.'" 1 SAMUEL 16:7

Time passed. Saul became proud and stubborn. He no longer obeyed God, and the Spirit left him. The Lord spoke to Samuel, "Go to the home of Jesse in Bethlehem. I have chosen one of his sons to be king." Samuel felt sorry for Saul. But he obeyed the Lord.

Samuel met seven of Jesse's sons. But God did
not choose any of them.
Samuel did not understand.
God told Samuel, "I don't look at how
handsome or tall a man is. I see a man's
heart and thoughts."

Samuel asked Jesse to send for his youngest
son, David, who was taking care of the sheep.
The Lord told Samuel to anoint David.
Samuel poured the oil on David's head.
The Lord's Spirit entered David. Samuel told
David that someday he would be king.

Meanwhile, King Saul was sad and worried
because God's Spirit was not with him.
Saul's servant said, "Send for David, the
shepherd. He sings and plays the harp. The
music will make you feel better."
Saul sent for David. And whenever David
sang and played, King Saul's sadness left him.

SONGS OF PRAISE

"Let everything that breathes praise the Lord." PSALM 150:6

David loved the Lord with all his heart.
He wrote many songs of praise while caring
for his sheep. He sang: "Lord, Your name is
the most wonderful name in all the earth.
Even children and babies sing praises to
You."

David wrote, "Children, come and listen to me. I will teach you to worship the Lord." He sang: "Every good thing I have comes from the Lord."
David said, "I praise the Lord at all times. His praise is always on my lips."

BIG MAN, LITTLE MAN

"'The Lord saved me from a lion and a bear. He will also save me from this Philistine. . . . The Lord does not need swords or spears to save people. The battle belongs to him! . . .'" 1 SAMUEL 17: 37, 47

"David!" Jesse called. "Take this bread and cheese to your big brothers. They are with Saul's army fighting against the evil Philistines.

Go, see how your brothers are doing. Then hurry home with your report."

Jesse knew he could trust David to obey him.

One of the Philistines was a giant man
named Goliath. Every day Goliath shouted,
"I dare any man in Israel to fight me! If your
man wins, then we will be your slaves. But if
I win, then you must be our slaves."

No man in Israel would stand up to Goliath.
David asked, "How can we let this man
shame God's army? I will fight Goliath."
Saul said, "You're just a boy."
"The Lord will save me from this giant,"
David answered.
Saul put his battle clothes on David, but the
boy couldn't move in them.

David took off Saul's armor.
Then, he picked five stones from a stream
and put them in a pouch.
David went to fight Goliath with his
shepherd's stick and his sling.
Goliath laughed, "Are you going to hit me
with your stick?"

David answered, "You come after me with a sword and spears. But I stand before you in the name of the Lord."
David put a stone into his sling and swung it around. The stone struck Goliath, and the giant fell to the ground. The Lord helped David win the victory.

A DANCE OF JOY

"David danced with all his might before the Lord. " 2 Samuel 6:14

David was a hero. Everyone loved him.
But Saul was very jealous.
Saul wanted to kill David so the people
couldn't make him king.
For many years, David hid from Saul.
And the Lord kept David safe.

When Saul died, David became king of
Israel. And he built a palace in Jerusalem.
The Holy Box of God was then moved to
Jerusalem. As the priests brought the Holy
Box into the city, the Israelites shouted for joy
and played their instruments. And David
danced with all his might before the Lord.

The Holy Box of God was put in a tent.
But King David said to Nathan the prophet,
"I want to build a temple for God."
That night, the Lord told Nathan, "Tell David
that his son will build My temple. And I will
make his kingdom last forever."

Nathan told David what God had said.
David praised God in the Holy Tent when he
heard this message.
"Lord, You have done great miracles for
Israel. And You have promised good things to
me, Your servant. Please, bless my family
forever!"

THE SPIRIT FILLS THE TEMPLE

"The Lord's glory filled the Temple." 2 Chronicles 7:1

Before David died, he told his son Solomon,
"Obey the Lord and you will be successful."
And that's what Solomon did.
Then the Lord came to Solomon in a dream.
God said, "Ask for anything, and I will give it
to you."
Solomon said, "Give me the wisdom to rule
Your people in the right way."

The Lord made King Solomon a wise ruler.
Then, Solomon built a house for God in
Jerusalem. It was called the temple.
The temple was like God's tent in the desert.
But it was much bigger and made of stone.
It sat high on a hilltop, called Mount Zion,
for everyone to see.

When the temple was completed, God's
people had a special service. The Holy Box
was placed in the Most Holy Place.
Everyone sang songs of praise.
The house of God filled with a cloud to show
the glory and presence of God.

King Solomon knelt to pray.
He asked God to bless the temple.
The Lord spoke to Solomon, "I have heard
your prayer. I have made this temple holy.
And I will bless this house as long as My
people obey Me!"

ELIJAH THE PROPHET

"The Lord, the God of Israel, says, 'That jar of flour will never become empty. The jug will always have oil in it. This will continue until the day the Lord sends rain to the land.'" 1 KINGS 17:14

While Solomon was king, Israel was a land of peace and great riches. But after Solomon died, the land was divided into the kingdoms of Israel and Judah.
Evil kings ruled for many years. Ahab was the worst king of all. He and his wicked wife, Jezebel, worshiped the false god Baal.

Ahab and Jezebel believed Baal ruled over the rain and sunshine.

Now, Elijah was a mighty prophet who served the true God of Israel. The Lord gave Elijah a message for Ahab: "There will be no rain in Israel until the Lord commands it." Ahab became very angry when he heard Elijah's words.

The Lord God led Elijah to a brook. God sent
birds with bread and meat for Elijah to eat.
Elijah drank water from the brook.
Many days passed without rain.
The plants died and the land became dry.
When the brook dried up, too, God sent
Elijah to the home of a poor widow.

Elijah asked the woman for a cup of water
and a piece of bread.
"All I have is enough flour and oil to make
one last meal for my son and me," she said.
"Bake me a small loaf of bread first," said
Elijah. "Then, cook for yourself."

"Don't worry," Elijah said. "Trust God to take care of you." The woman shared her little bit of bread with Elijah, and the Lord blessed her with more. The jar of flour and the jug of oil were never empty. So Elijah, the widow, and her son had enough food for each day.

VICTORY ON MOUNT CARMEL

"Elijah stood before the people. He said, 'How long will you try to serve both Baal and the Lord? If the Lord is the true God, follow him. But if Baal is the true God, follow him!'" 1 KINGS 18:21

There was no rain in Israel for three years. The people had no food. One day Elijah told Ahab that God would send rain soon.
Ahab called Elijah "Israel's troublemaker." But Elijah said, "You're the cause of Israel's hunger. You disobeyed God by telling His people to bow before Baal."

Elijah told Ahab to meet him on Mount
Carmel. Elijah also invited all Israel and the
prophets of Baal. Elijah told the people, "You
can't serve both God and Baal."
He told the prophets of Baal, "Build two
altars. You offer a sacrifice to Baal, and I will
offer a sacrifice to the Lord."

Then Elijah said, "You pray to your god and I
will pray to the Lord. The god who answers
with fire is the true God."
The prophets of Baal built an altar. But when
they prayed, nothing happened. Baal did not
speak because he was only a statue.

Elijah built an altar. He poured water on the
stones, the wood, and the sacrifice.
Elijah prayed, "Lord, I ask You to show these
people that You are God."
Fire came down from heaven. It burned up
the sacrifice, the wood, the stones, and the
water. When the people saw this, they cried
"The Lord, He is God!"
Elijah prayed again, and the Lord sent rain.

A WIND AND A WHISPER

*"Then a very strong wind blew. . . . But the Lord was not in the wind. . . .
After the fire, there was a quiet, gentle voice."* 1 KINGS 19:11, 12

Queen Jezebel was angry because God had
answered Elijah's prayer.
She sent Elijah a message: "Tomorrow you
will die." Elijah ran away to save his life. He
walked through a desert for one whole day.
He was tired and hungry. At last he lay down
and fell asleep.

The Lord was kind to Elijah. Twice, He sent
an angel to cheer him up.
The angel touched him and said, "Get up
and eat, Elijah. If you don't, the trip will be
too hard for you."
Elijah opened his eyes and saw a loaf of
bread and a jug of water. The food made him
strong enough to walk for forty more days.

Finally, Elijah came to Mount Sinai, the mountain of God. The Lord said, "Stand in front of Me. I will pass by you."
A great wind swept by Elijah, but the Lord was not in it. Elijah saw an earthquake, but the Lord was not in it. A fire passed by, too, but the Lord was not in it, either.

After the fire, Elijah heard a soft voice. He
knew it was the voice of the Lord.
"Why are you running, Elijah?" the Lord
asked him.
"I feel afraid and alone," Elijah said.
The Lord said, "Go pour oil on Elisha. He will
be your helper."

THE BATTLE IS THE LORD'S

"The Lord says this to you: 'Don't be afraid or discouraged. . . . The battle is not your battle. It is God's battle. . . .'" 2 CHRONICLES 20:15

During the days of Elijah, there lived a good king named Jehoshaphat.
The Lord was with Jehoshaphat because he obeyed God's commands. Jehoshaphat removed the false gods in Judah. Then he sent out priests to teach the people how to serve the Lord.

One day, a large army wanted to fight God's people. Jehoshaphat called the people to a special time of prayer.
He told the people not to eat any food that day. People traveled from every town in Judah to pray with Jehoshaphat in Jerusalem.

Jehoshaphat prayed, "Lord, we have no power against this army. Please, help us." Then the Spirit entered the man Jahaziel. Jahaziel said, "Don't be afraid for the Lord is with you. You will not have to fight. The battle is the Lord's."

The people worshiped the Lord.

The next morning, Jehoshaphat said to his
army, "Believe in the Lord and you will stand
strong." As the army of Judah marched
toward the enemy, they sang and praised
God. Then God caused the enemy soldiers to
fight each other. So God's people won the
battle without fighting.

King Jehoshaphat and his people gathered
everything the enemy left behind. They
carried away money, jewelry, and clothes.
The people praised the Lord for His help and
blessing. They were happy because their
enemies were defeated.

THE CHARIOT OF FIRE

"A group of the prophets at Jericho were watching. They said, 'Elisha now has the spirit Elijah had.'" 2 KINGS 2:15

The work of Elijah was finished. He would soon be taken to heaven.
His helper Elisha walked with him to the Jordan River. Elijah took off his coat. He rolled it up and hit the water.
The water divided to the right and left. They crossed over on dry ground.

Elijah said to Elisha, "What can I do for you before I go to heaven?"

Elisha wanted to inherit Elijah's power from God. Elisha said, "Please leave me a double share of your spirit."

"You have asked for a special gift," Elijah said.

Then Elijah said, "If you see me leave, the power from the Spirit will be given to you." Suddenly a chariot and horses of fire appeared. Elisha watched as the chariot took Elijah to heaven in a whirlwind. Elisha did not see his friend anymore. But Elijah had dropped his coat. So Elisha picked it up.

Elisha walked to the Jordan River.
He hit the water with Elijah's coat.
The water parted just as it had for Elijah.
Elisha now had the same power that Elijah
had used. The Lord had chosen Elisha to
replace the great prophet Elijah.

A DEAD BOY SNEEZES

"When Elisha entered the room, he shut the door. Only he and the child were in the room. Then Elisha prayed to the Lord. . . . The child sneezed seven times and opened his eyes." 2 KINGS 4:33, 35

Elisha traveled throughout Israel. He taught the people to worship the Lord.
In one city, a wealthy woman invited Elisha to her home for dinner. Whenever Elisha passed through that city, he visited the woman and her husband.

183

Later, the woman and her husband built a small room on the roof for Elisha. They put a bed, a chair, a table, and a lampstand in it. Now Elisha had a place to rest.

One day, Elisha said to the woman, "What can
I do for you? You have been so kind to me."
The woman said, "There is nothing I need."
Elisha said to her, "God will give you a son
next year."
And Elisha's words came true.

Several years later, the woman's child cried,
"My head hurts!"
The sick boy died in his mother's arms.
The woman sadly carried him into Elisha's
room. Then, she quickly saddled the donkey
and hurried to find Elisha.

When the boy's mother reached Elisha, she
cried for her son. She said, "Elisha, I won't
leave unless you come with me!"
So, Elisha followed her home. Elisha prayed
over the boy. The child sneezed seven times
and opened his eyes. The woman praised the
Lord for bringing her son back to life.

A LITTLE GIRL HELPS

"Naaman . . . stood before Elisha and said, 'Look. I now know there is no God in all the earth except in Israel!'" 2 KINGS 5:15

Naaman was a hero and leader of a foreign army. But an ugly disease covered his skin. Naaman and his wife had an Israelite servant. One day, the little servant girl said, "I wish my master would meet the prophet Elisha. He could heal Naaman."

Naaman listened to the little girl.
He traveled many miles to Elisha's home in
Israel. He waited at Elisha's door. But the
prophet didn't come.
Instead, Elisha sent a messenger to speak
with Naaman.

The messenger said, "Wash in the Jordan River seven times and you will be healed." Naaman was a proud man. He was upset that Elisha did not talk to him. One of Naaman's servants said gently, "Sir, the prophet didn't ask you to do something difficult. He said to wash, and you will be well."

So Naaman dipped seven times in the Jordan River. His skin became healthy. He hurried back to Elisha's house.

"Look! Your God healed me," Naaman told Elisha. "I will serve no other God, but the Lord."

THE BIG FISH NEAR TARSHISH

" 'Lord, I will praise and thank you while I give sacrifices to you. I will make promises to you. And I will do what I promise. Salvation comes from the Lord!' " JONAH 2:9

After Elisha died, God spoke to another prophet. His name was Jonah.
"Go to Ninevah, the great city in Assyria," God said. "Preach to the people."

Jonah did not want to preach to his enemies.
So he ran away from the Lord.
He boarded a ship to Tarshish. Then Jonah
fell asleep, thinking he was safe.
But the Lord sent a great storm while the ship
was at sea. The ship was about to sink.
The terrified sailors prayed to their gods.

The captain woke Jonah, "Get up! Pray to
your God! Maybe He will save us!"
Jonah said, "It's my fault this storm has
come. I ran away from God. Throw me into
the water and the storm will stop."
So they threw Jonah into the sea.
And the water became calm.

The men on the ship greatly feared Jonah's God. They promised to serve the Lord. Meanwhile, Jonah cried for God to save him. And the Lord caused a big fish to swallow him up.

Jonah lived inside the fish for three days. There he praised the Lord for saving his life.

Jonah promised to obey God.
Then the Lord caused the fish to spit him out
onto dry land.
Jonah took God's word to the people of
Ninevah.
The people turned away from their sins and
believed in the Lord.

THE KING OF JUDAH

" 'Don't be afraid of what you have heard. Don't be frightened. . . .'"
2 Kings 19: 6

Many years passed. Hezekiah became the
king of Judah. He obeyed the Lord.
Hezekiah helped the people remember their
promises to God, and the Lord blessed them.

One time the Assyrian army marched toward
Jerusalem. So God's people built stronger
walls around the city.
Hezekiah told the people, "Don't be afraid.
God is with us."

God's people watched from the walls as the
enemy army surrounded their city.
The enemy captain yelled, "Don't listen to
Hezekiah. Your God can't save you!"
Hezekiah told his people, "Don't answer
him." The people kept quiet.
Then Hezekiah went to the temple to pray.

Hezekiah called for Isaiah the prophet.
Isaiah said, "Don't be scared. The Lord will
defend and save you."
That night, God sent an angel to attack and
kill the enemy. So the Lord saved Hezekiah
and the people of Judah.

HEZEKIAH'S HEALING

". . . The Lord, the God of your ancestor David, says: 'I have heard your prayer. And I have seen your tears. So I will heal you. . . . '"
2 KINGS 20:5

Hezekiah became sick with a deadly disease. Isaiah said, "Get ready to die. The Lord says you won't get better."
Hezekiah cried to the Lord, "God, please remember how I've always tried to obey You." He begged God to give him a longer life.

God gave Isaiah a message for Hezekiah.
Isaiah said, "You will be healed. The Lord
will add many years to your life."
Isaiah told Hezekiah to put medicine on his
body. Then Isaiah prayed for Hezekiah, and
he was healed.

THE BOY KING

" 'You became sorry in the Lord's presence for what you had done . . . This is why I have heard you, says the Lord.' " 2 KINGS 22:19

Before long, the people of Judah turned from
God to fortune-tellers and witchcraft.
At this time, Josiah became king.
He was only eight years old!
But he loved the Lord and tried to live right.

When Josiah was old enough to rule, he
hired workers to fix up God's house.
One day, the workers found an old scroll that
had been lost for many years.
A priest took it to Josiah. "Here's a book of
God's rules!" the priest said. Then a servant
read God's Word to Josiah.

Josiah was very upset.
His people were not following God's rules!
"Ask God what we should do," Josiah told the
priest. The priest went to Huldah, a prophetess.
Huldah gave him God's message. "The people
have sinned. But the Lord will not harm
Josiah because he is sorry for their sins."

Josiah called all the people to the temple.
He read the book of God's rules for everyone
to hear. Then the people promised to obey
God's Word. And they destroyed all their
false gods.
There was never another king like Josiah.
He obeyed the Lord with all his heart.

A PROPHET WHO CRIED

"The Lord says . . . 'You will . . . pray to me. And I will listen to you. . . . When you search for me with all your heart, you will find me!'" JEREMIAH 29: 10-13

Jeremiah was a prophet of God.
The Lord gave him a sad message to give to the people of Jerusalem.
"Soon the king of Babylon will capture you."
But the people didn't listen.

One day King Nebuchadnezzar came from
Babylon with his mighty army.
He attacked Jerusalem.
He took the temple treasures and many of
the people to Babylon.
Jeremiah cried when God's words came true.

Jeremiah wrote a letter to comfort the prisoners in Babylon.

He told them, "The Lord says: 'I will change your sadness into joy. I will bring you back to Jerusalem when you learn to follow Me with all your heart.'"

THE FIRE PIT

"Then Nebuchadnezzar said . . . 'These three men . . . were willing to die rather than serve or worship any god other than their own. . . . No other god can save his people like this.'" Daniel 3:28, 29

In Babylon, King Nebuchadnezzar asked for four young men from Judah to serve in his palace. Daniel and his three friends were chosen. They studied hard to learn the king's language. And God helped them.

King Nebuchadnezzar had a huge gold statue
made. He ordered everyone in Babylon to
bow down and worship the statue.
"Anyone who doesn't will be thrown into a
fire pit," the king said.
Daniel's three friends would not bow and
worship the golden statue.

When the king found out, he was very angry.
He called for Shadrach, Meshach, and
Abednego.
"Why won't you worship my statue?" the
king asked.
They answered, "We worship only God."
So the king had them thrown into a fire pit.

When the king looked into the pit, he saw
four men instead of three. They were walking
around in the fire and were not burned.
"The fourth man looks like a son of the gods,"
the king said. "Praise the God of Shadrach,
Meshach, and Abednego.
He has saved them from the fire."

A SECRET MESSAGE

"The Most High God rules over the kingdoms of men. And the Most High God sets anyone he wants over those kingdoms." DANIEL 5:21

Many years later, the king's son had a big party to honor the false gods.
He used golden cups that were stolen from the Lord's temple.
Suddenly the hand of God wrote a message on the wall. Everyone was afraid.

The wise men in the kingdom could not
understand the writing.
So the king's son sent for Daniel because he
knew how to explain dreams.
"If you can read this writing, I will give you a
great reward," the king told Daniel.
"Please, keep your gifts," Daniel said.

"You have offended the Most High God,"
Daniel told the king's son. "You have used His
holy things in a wrong way. God has sent this
message to tell you your kingdom will be
taken away from you."
And God's words came true.

DANIEL IN THE LIONS' PIT

"Then King Darius wrote . . . . 'All of you must fear and respect the God of Daniel. . . . God saved Daniel from the power of the lion.'" DANIEL 6:25–27

The next ruler was King Darius. He knew
Daniel was wise and truthful. He chose
Daniel to help him rule the kingdom.
The other leaders were jealous.
They thought of a way to trap Daniel.

These men knew Daniel prayed to the Lord
each day. So they tricked the king into
signing a law about prayer.
It said no one should pray to any god but
King Darius!
Anyone who disobeyed the law would be
thrown into the lions' pit.

Daniel heard about the law, but it did not
stop him from praying to God.
The men told the king about Daniel.
The king was very sad and upset.
He didn't want to punish his loyal helper.
But he couldn't change the foolish law.
Daniel was thrown into the lions' pit.

The next morning Darius hurried to the lions' pit. He called, "Daniel, has the God you worship been able to save you?"

"Yes," Daniel answered. "God sent an angel to close the lions' mouths."

Then Darius said, "I'm making a new law. People in my kingdom must fear your God."

A BEAUTY QUEEN

"'You may have been chosen queen for just such a time as this.'"
ESTHER 4:14

The king of Persia needed a queen.
All the prettiest girls in the kingdom were
brought before him.
Esther was the most beautiful girl of all.
She was chosen to be the queen.

No one in the palace knew Esther was Jewish.
"Keep it secret," said Esther's Uncle Mordecai.
Esther always listened to his wise advice.
One day Haman, the king's officer, came to
the city. Everyone bowed down.
But Mordecai would not bow.
He worshiped only the Lord God.

Haman hated Mordecai the Jew.
He made an evil plan to get rid of him.
He tricked the king into signing a law to kill
all the Jewish people living in the land.
Mordecai asked Esther to talk to the king.
Esther said, "There is a law that forbids me
from going to the king without being invited.
I could be punished."

Mordecai said, "God may have let you be chosen queen for just such a time as this. Help your people."

Esther prayed for courage. Then she boldly went to see the king. The king loved Esther and listened to her.

He punished Haman instead of Mordecai or Esther. So God used Esther to save her people.

DOUBLE TROUBLE

"'The Lord gave these things to me. And he has taken them away. Praise the name of the Lord.'" JOB 1: 21

Job was a good man. He tried to live right.
He prayed every day, "Lord, help me obey
You. Please forgive my sins."
God was pleased with Job and blessed him.
Job was one of the richest men in the world.
Job had eleven grown children. He owned a
large farm with many animals and servants.

Satan hated Job for serving the Lord.
One day, Satan stole everything from Job.
Wild men robbed his farm.
The animals were stolen.
His servants were killed.
A tornado took the lives of all his children.
Job lost all he had.

Even though he was sad, Job praised God.
Then Satan caused Job to become sick.
Job's wife said bitterly, "You should blame
God for all this trouble!"
Job said, "Should we take only good things
from God? I don't understand my troubles,
but I won't blame God. I will keep on trusting
Him."

Job said to God, "I know You can do all
things."
After that God healed Job's body. And once
again God blessed Job with many animals,
servants, sons, and daughters.
Job was richer and happier now than he
had been before all his troubles.

REBUILDING THE CITY

"The joy of the Lord will make you strong." NEHEMIAH *8:10*

After many years the king of Persia told
God's people, "You may go back to your
homeland and rebuild God's temple!"
The king returned all the valuable treasures
that had been stolen from God's house.
As the people traveled to Jerusalem, they
praised God for keeping His promises.

When they arrived in Jerusalem, God's
people found their city in ruins.
The walls had fallen. The temple was wrecked.
The people were eager to rebuild God's
House. They rebuilt the altar and laid the
temple base. But soon they grew tired and
stopped working.

The Lord spoke to His people through two
men named Haggai and Zechariah.
Haggai told the people, "You have forgotten
God's House. Be brave and work for the
Lord."
Then Zechariah said, "Remember, you won't
do well using your own strength. The power
comes from the Holy Spirit."

The people finished the temple.
But they left the city walls undone.
God caused a man named Nehemiah to
want to rebuild the walls of Jerusalem.
Nehemiah spoke to all the people,
"We are helpless against enemy attacks
without strong walls around our city.
Let's work together to rebuild them."

So each family rebuilt the part of the wall
closest to their home. People outside the city
tried to stop the work on the walls.
They tried to scare the workers.
Nehemiah prayed for God's help.
He chose watchmen to walk around the walls
and guard against enemies.

After fifty-two days of hard work, Jerusalem was a strong, walled city. Then God's people celebrated for seven days. Each day, Ezra, the teacher, read God's Word to them. And they confessed their sins and prayed with loud voices: "You are the only Lord."

The people gave God a tenth of everything
they had earned. Then everyone marched
around the city on top of the walls, singing
and praising God with great joy.
They finally understood what they had been
taught.

New Testament

*"**G**od will give a son to us. . . . His name will be Wonderful Counselor, Powerful God, Father Who Lives Forever, Prince of Peace. . . . He will rule as king on David's throne."*

—Isaiah 9:6,7

AN ANGEL VISITS MARY

"God has done what he promised." LUKE 1:55

Mary was a young Jewish girl engaged to
Joseph, the carpenter.
Joseph was a good man who loved the Lord.
He would make a fine husband for Mary.
Soon, all their friends and family would
celebrate the wedding in Nazareth.
But Mary's life was about to change forever.

One day, God sent an angel to Mary. The
angel said, "Don't be afraid. God is pleased
with you. He has chosen you to be the
mother of Jesus. This Holy Child will be the
King that God promised. And He will be
called the Son of God."

Mary did not understand.
The angel said, "The Holy Spirit will make this happen."
Then he said, "Everyone thought your cousin Elizabeth could not have children.
But she will have a baby in her old age.
God will do everything He promised!"

Mary hurried to Elizabeth and Zechariah's home.

When Elizabeth heard Mary's voice, her unborn baby jumped for joy. And Elizabeth was filled with the Holy Spirit.

She said, "Mary, you are blessed because you believed what God said."

Mary was filled with joy and sang a song:
"My soul praises the Lord; my heart is happy
because God is my Savior."
Mary stayed with Elizabeth and Zechariah
for three months.

ZECHARIAH'S PROPHECY

" 'Now you, child, will be called a prophet of the Most High God. . . . You will make his people know that they will be saved . . . by having their sins forgiven.' " LUKE 1:76–77

Several months before Mary's visit, an angel spoke to Zechariah, the priest.
"Your wife, Elizabeth, will give birth to a son. And you will name him John."
Zechariah was surprised!

The angel said, "John will help people get
ready for the coming of the Lord."
Zechariah doubted. He said, "My wife and I
are very old. Are you sure?"
The angel answered, "Because you didn't
believe, you will lose your speech until
Elizabeth has the baby."

When the baby was born, everyone expected him to be named Zechariah, after his father. But Elizabeth said, "No! He will be named John."

Their friends said, "No one in your family has that name!"

They asked Zechariah what to call his son.

Zechariah could not speak, so he wrote, "His name is John." Everyone was shocked! Suddenly Zechariah started talking and praising God. He was filled with the Holy Spirit and said, "This child will be a prophet of God. He will point the people to the Savior."

GOD BECAME A BABY BOY

"All the angels were praising God, saying: 'Give glory to God in heaven, and on earth let there be peace to the people who please God.'" LUKE 2:13–14

One night, an angel came to Joseph in a dream. "Don't be afraid to take Mary as your wife. The baby inside her is from the Holy Spirit," the angel said. "You will call Him Jesus, which means, *The Lord Saves.*"
So Joseph and Mary were married.

The emperor said that all the people must go to their birthplaces to list their names and to pay taxes.

Joseph and Mary traveled many miles to Bethlehem, their hometown. Mary was very tired, but there was no place to rest.

Bethlehem was crowded with people.
And Mary and Joseph had to spend the
night in a stable.
During the night, Mary's baby was born.
Mary loved her wonderful Son.
She wrapped Him in warm clothes and made
a cozy bed for Him in a feedbox.

Some shepherds were watching their sheep in a nearby field. Suddenly an angel appeared. The shepherds were frightened.

The angel said, "Don't be afraid. I am bringing you good news. Tonight your Savior was born in Bethlehem. He is CHRIST the Lord."

Then a choir of angels sang, "Glory to God in heaven."

When the angels left, the shepherds hurried to Bethlehem. They found the baby with Mary and Joseph.

The shepherds were amazed!

They returned to the fields, praising God.

SIMEON PRAISES GOD

"The Holy Spirit told Simeon that he would not die before he saw the Christ." LUKE 2:26

Mary and Joseph took Jesus to the temple. An old man named Simeon was there. He was looking for the coming Savior. Simeon praised God when he saw Jesus with Mary and Joseph.

Simeon took Jesus in his arms and said,
"Lord, now I can die in peace. I have seen
the Savior."
An old prophetess named Anna heard
Simeon.
When Anna saw Jesus, she told everyone
that God's promised King had come.

WISE MEN WORSHIP

"When the wise men saw the star, they were filled with joy. They went to the house where the child was. . . . They bowed down and worshiped the child." MATTHEW *2:10, 11*

Mary and Joseph returned to Bethlehem.
Special visitors came from a faraway land to worship Jesus.
They had seen a strange star shining in the sky.

These wise men believed the star meant a
king was born. So they followed the star to
the place where the child was.
The wise men were filled with joy.
They bowed down and worshiped Jesus.
They gave Him precious, costly gifts.

LOST AND FOUND

"The little child began to grow up. He became stronger and wiser, and God's blessings were with him." LUKE *2:40*

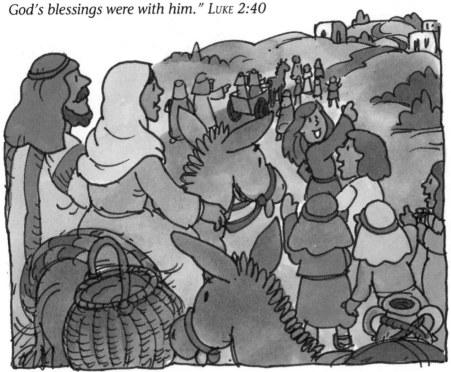

When Jesus was twelve, He went with Joseph and Mary to Jerusalem. They went for the Passover Feast. After the celebration, many people traveled home together. But Jesus stayed behind in the city. Joseph and Mary did not know it.

Joseph and Mary traveled a whole day before
they realized Jesus was missing.
They went back to Jerusalem to look for Him.
After three days they found Jesus.
He was in the temple, talking to the teachers.

All who heard Jesus were amazed at His
understanding. But Mary and Joseph were
upset. His mother said to Him, "Son, we've
been looking for You! Why did You worry us?"
Jesus said, "Why did you have to look for Me?
You should have known I'd be in my Father's
House."
Jesus went home with Mary and Joseph.
He obeyed them and pleased God.

BAPTIZED!

"'I baptize you with water to show that your hearts and lives have changed. But there is one coming later who is greater than I am. . . . He will baptize you with the Holy Spirit and with fire.'" MATTHEW *3:11*

John was the son of Zechariah and Elizabeth. He was no ordinary man. John lived alone in the desert so he could hear the voice of God. He ate wild honey and locusts.
God gave John a message for the people.

Crowds came to hear John preach.
He said, "Turn away from your sins.
Get ready to meet the Son of God."
John told the people to stop stealing and
lying. He said, "Share with people who are
poor and hungry."

John baptized people in the Jordan River.
Many people thought John might be God's
promised King.
John said, "I am not the Savior. I baptize
you with water. But He will baptize you with
the Holy Spirit."

THE DOVE FROM ABOVE

"John said, 'I saw the Spirit come down from heaven. The Spirit looked like a dove and rested on him . . . So I tell people: 'He is the Son of God.'" JOHN 1: 33, 34

Jesus came to John to be baptized. John said, "Look! Here comes the One I've been talking about. He will take away the sins of the world." John was not sure he should be the one to baptize Jesus. But Jesus said, "This is God's plan."

John agreed to baptize Jesus.
When Jesus came up out of the water, the
Holy Spirit came down in the form of a dove
and rested on Him.
Then God's voice spoke from heaven, "You
are My Son and I love You."

DOWN WITH THE DEVIL!

"Jesus said to the devil, 'Go away from me, Satan!' . . . So the devil left Jesus. And then some angels came to Jesus and helped him." MATTHEW *4:10, 11*

The Spirit led Jesus into the desert to pray. For forty days Jesus did not eat. When Jesus was tired and hungry, the Devil tried to get Him to disobey God.

The Devil said, "If You are God's Son, change these stones into bread, and eat."

Jesus said, "The Scripture says, 'There are things in life more important than food.'" The Devil told Jesus, "I will give You everything in the world if You worship me." Jesus answered, "God's Word says, 'You must worship and serve Him only.'"

Satan said, "Prove that You are God's Son.
Jump off the temple roof. God's Word says
His angels will catch You."
Jesus said, "The Scripture also says, 'Don't
test God's power foolishly.'"
Jesus did not disobey God. So, Satan left Him.
Then God sent His angels to feed Jesus.

THE FIRST MIRACLE

"His mother said to the servants, 'Do whatever he tells you to do.'"
JOHN 2:5

Jesus went to a wedding with His mother,
Mary, and some friends. There wasn't enough
wine for the feast. And the bridegroom was
upset.
Mary asked Jesus to help.
Jesus said, "Why come to Me?"

But His mother trusted Jesus to do the right thing. She told the servants, "Do whatever Jesus tells you to do."
Jesus told the servants to fill six big jars with water. When the bridegroom tasted the water, he was surprised. The water had become wine. This was Jesus' first miracle.

FOLLOWING JESUS

"At that time Jesus went off to a mountain to pray. He stayed there all night, praying to God. The next morning, Jesus called his followers to him. He chose 12 of them." LUKE 6:12–13

Jesus went to the synagogue.
He read God's Word to the people.
He said, "The Spirit of the Lord is in Me. God has chosen Me to tell the Good News. He has sent Me to help the sinners and to heal those who are hurting." Then Jesus began to explain God's Word to the people.

One day a crowd of people followed Jesus to
Lake Galilee.
Jesus saw two boats near the shore. The
boats belonged to a group of fishermen—
Peter, Andrew, James, and John.
The men were washing their fishing nets.

Jesus got into Peter's boat and taught the people on the shore. Later, Jesus told Peter, "Put your nets in the deep water, and you will catch fish."

Peter said, "Master, we tried all night, and we didn't catch any fish." But Peter and the other fishermen obeyed Jesus anyway.

They caught so many fish that their nets broke. The fishermen were amazed.

Peter bowed before Jesus and said, "Lord, why bother with me? I am a sinner."

Jesus answered, "From now on you will fish for men."

The men left their boats and followed Jesus.

Jesus chose twelve men to be His closest
friends: Peter and his brother Andrew;
James and his brother John; Philip and
Nathaniel; Matthew, the tax-collector;
Thomas; James, the son of Alphaeus;
Simon; Thaddaeus; and Judas. These
men followed Jesus everywhere.

HEALING THE SICK

"Jesus saw that these men believed. So he said to the sick man, 'Friend, your sins are forgiven.'" LUKE 5:20

Jesus was teaching and healing people in a crowded house. Several Jewish leaders were there. They were jealous because Jesus had so many followers.

A paralyzed man could not move from
his bed.
Four good friends carried him to the house
where Jesus was preaching. But the house
was so full of people there was no place to
lay the man.

The friends lowered the man through a hole in the roof.

Jesus told the paralyzed man, "Your sins are forgiven."

The Jewish leaders became angry.

"Only God can forgive sins. Who does Jesus think He is?"

Jesus proved He had the power to forgive
sins. He told the paralyzed man, "Get up.
Take your mat and go home."
The healed man stood up and walked out of
the room.
The people were amazed and praised God.

PREACHING AND TEACHING

" 'The thing you should want most is God's kingdom and doing what God wants. Then all these other things you need will be given to you.' "
MATTHEW *6:33*

One day Jesus sat on a hillside and taught His followers.
"See the birds in the sky? Your heavenly Father feeds them. God helps the lovely flowers to grow, too."

"If God cares about the birds and flowers, you can trust Him to take care of you," He said. "Remember, the most important thing is to love God and to do what He wants. You please Him by showing love and kindness to others."

"Everyone who obeys Me is like the wise man who built his house on rock," Jesus said. "The rain poured, the water rose, and the wind beat against the house. But the house did not fall because it was built on rock."

"The person who does not obey Me is like a foolish man who built his house on sand," Jesus said.
"When the storm came, the water rose, and the wind hit the house. The house fell with a big crash."

BORN AGAIN

"'For God loved the world so much that he gave his only Son. God gave his Son so that whoever believes in him may not be lost, but have eternal life.'" John 3:16

Nicodemus was an important Jewish leader. He wanted to talk to Jesus, but he didn't want any of his friends to see him.
So he came to Jesus in secret at night.
Jesus knew Nicodemus didn't understand God's plan.

Jesus told Nicodemus, "You must be born again if you want to go to heaven."
"How can a man be born twice?" Nicodemus asked.
Jesus explained, "The Holy Spirit will give you a new life. Everyone who believes in Me as Savior will go to heaven."

JESUS PUTS AWAY THE DEMONS

"The man that Jesus had healed begged to go with him. But Jesus sent him away, saying, 'Go back home and tell people what God did for you.'" LUKE 8:38–39

A man with many demons came to Jesus. This man lived in a cave and wore no clothes. When he saw Jesus, he fell to his knees.

Jesus commanded the evil spirit to come out of the man. When Jesus did this, the demons came out of the man and went into some pigs that were eating nearby.
All the pigs ran into a lake and drowned.

The men who took care of the pigs ran to town and told everyone what had happened. The people in town came to see if the crazy man was cured. He was!
He was listening to Jesus teach.

A TOUCH OF FAITH

"Jesus said . . . 'You are made well because you believed. Go in peace. You will have no more suffering.'" Mark 5:34

A man named Jairus bowed before Jesus and begged, "Please heal my little girl. She's dying!" Jesus went with Jairus, and many people followed.

In the crowd was a woman with a blood
disease. No one could cure her.
The woman had heard about Jesus' miracles.
She believed Jesus could heal her if she could
just reach Him through the crowd.

The woman came up behind Jesus as He
walked with Jairus. She touched the edge of
Jesus' coat.
Instantly, she was healed.
"Who touched Me?" asked Jesus.
Peter said, "Master, anyone in this crowd
could have touched You."

The frightened woman stepped forward.
Jesus said, "You are healed because you
believed."
At the same time, a messenger hurried to
Jairus. "Your daughter is dead!" he cried.
Jesus told Jairus, "Don't be afraid; only believe."

At Jairus's house, everyone was crying.
Jesus said, "Don't cry. The girl is sleeping."
The people laughed at Jesus.
Jesus told the unbelievers to leave the room.
Jesus held the girl's hand and said, "My
child, stand up!" Jairus's daughter stood up.
She was well!

WEEDS AND SEEDS

"Jesus said, 'You have been chosen to know the secret truths of the kingdom of God.'" LUKE 8:10

Jesus told many stories about God's kingdom. "A farmer went out to plant seed," Jesus said. "As he scattered the seed, some fell beside the road. The birds came and ate it all."

"Some seeds fell on rocky ground," He said.
"The hot sun burned those little plants
because they had short roots. Other seeds fell
among weeds that would later choke the
growing plants. But, the seeds that fell on
good soil grew into strong, healthy plants."

The people asked, "What does this story
mean?"
Jesus explained, "The seed is the word of
God. Some people hear His word; then Satan
steals it from them. Other people listen but
give up easily when problems come."

"Others let worries and love of money crowd
God from their hearts," Jesus said.
"The people who understand God's message
are like the seeds planted on good soil. They
grow into beautiful 'plants.' Then they tell
others the Good News."

TWELVE APOSTLES SENT OUT

"'When you go, preach this: 'The kingdom of heaven is coming soon.' Heal the sick. Give dead people life again. Heal those who have harmful skin diseases. Force demons to leave people.'" MATTHEW 10:7–8

Jesus' twelve closest followers were called apostles.

He gave them power to heal all sicknesses and to drive out demons.

"I give you this gift freely," Jesus said.

"So help other people freely."

Jesus said, "Go and tell the people about
God's kingdom.
Give dead people life again. Heal the sick.
Don't worry about what to say. The Spirit of
God will give you the right words."

The apostles told people to turn away from their sins and live right.
The twelve men poured olive oil on sick people, and God healed them. Jesus was pleased.

A BUNCH FOR LUNCH

"All the people ate and were satisfied. And there was much food left."
LUKE *9:17*

One day Jesus and His friends sailed across
Lake Galilee. Then they went up on a hill
and sat down.
Many people followed Jesus.
He felt sorry for them because they were like
sheep without a shepherd.

Jesus taught the people all day long.
He said, "Heaven is like a beautiful pearl.
It's worth more than anything else."
After a while, Jesus told His apostles to feed
the people.
Philip answered, "It would take a lot of
money to buy food for this crowd!"

One little boy had five loaves of bread and two little fish.

He gave them to Andrew.

Andrew told Jesus, "This boy will share his meal, but it's not enough."

Jesus said, "Tell all the people to sit down for dinner."

Jesus took the bread and fish.
He looked up to heaven and thanked God.
Then Jesus divided the food and gave it to His
followers. And they shared it with the hungry
people. Everyone had plenty of food to eat.
There were twelve baskets of food left over.

WALKING ON WATER

"Jesus quickly spoke to them. He said, 'Have courage! It is I! Don't be afraid.'" Matthew 14:27

After Jesus fed the large crowd, He sent His apostles by boat to the other side of the lake. Jesus stayed behind until everyone went home. Then He went into the hills to pray.

During the night, a storm came up.
The men in the boat worried that they might
sink. Suddenly a man appeared. He was
walking toward them on the water!
"It's a ghost!" the men cried.
"It is I!" said Jesus. "Do not be afraid."

Peter said, "Lord, can I walk on water, too?"
Jesus said, "Come!"
Peter slowly stepped toward Jesus.
Peter felt the blowing wind and saw the high
waves around him.
He became frightened and started to sink.

"Lord, save me!" Peter cried.
Jesus quickly rescued Peter.
"Why did you doubt?" Jesus asked Peter.
When Jesus and Peter got into the boat, the
wind became calm.
"You truly are the Son of God!" said the men.

SEE HIS GLORY

"Then a cloud came and covered them. A voice came from the cloud. The voice said, 'This is my Son, and I love him. Obey him!'" Mark 9:7

Jesus took Peter, James, and John up on a mountain to pray. While Jesus was praying, a great change came over Him.
His face began to shine like the sun, and His clothes became whiter than snow.
His friends saw the glory of Jesus.

Suddenly Moses and Elijah appeared with
Jesus. Jesus' followers were frightened, and a
cloud covered them.
A voice from the cloud said, "This is My Son.
He is the One I have chosen. Obey Him."

A BLIND MAN SEES

"One thing I do know. I was blind, and now I can see.'" JOHN *9:25*

One day Jesus saw a blind man.
"Why was he born blind?" asked Jesus'
followers. "Was it his sins or his parents'
sins?"
"Neither," Jesus answered. "He was born
blind so God's power could be shown in him."

Jesus put mud on the man's eyes and said,
"Go and wash in the Pool of Siloam."
The blind man washed in the water.
He could see!
Several people asked him, "Are you the blind
beggar? How did you get your sight?"

He answered, "Jesus healed me!"
When the Jewish leaders heard his story,
they did not believe it.
They asked his parents if he really had been
born blind.

Again they asked the man, "What happened?"
He answered, "All I know is that once I was
blind, and now I can see!"
The Jewish leaders threw him out of the temple.
Jesus found the man and asked him, "Do you
believe in Me?"
"Yes, Lord, I believe!" the man said.

THE GOOD NEIGHBOR

"'Love the Lord your God. Love him with all your heart, all your soul, all your strength, and all your mind. Also, you must love your neighbor as you love yourself.'" LUKE 10:27

A Jewish lawyer asked Jesus, "What must I do to go to heaven?"

"What does God's law say?" asked Jesus.

"Love the Lord with all your heart and your neighbor as yourself," he answered.

"You are right," said Jesus.

"But, who is my neighbor?" asked the lawyer.

Jesus told him a story.
"Once a traveler was attacked by robbers.
They beat him and left him to die in a ditch.
Then a priest passed by. But when he saw the
injured man, he walked by on the other side
of the road," said Jesus.

"Next a temple worker hurried by.
He didn't stop to help, either.
Finally, a foreigner saw the poor man.
He bandaged the man's wounds.
Then he lifted the man out of the ditch and
took him to a safe place."

Jesus asked the lawyer, "Which man was a good neighbor to the hurting stranger?" "The man who helped him," said the lawyer. Jesus said, "Go and do the same thing. Take care of the hurting people around you."

THE LOST SON

"The son said, 'Father, I have sinned against God and have done wrong to you. I am not good enough to be called your son.'" Luke 15:21

Jesus told a story about a man with two sons. One son said, "Father, I want my share of your wealth while I'm still young!"
So the father divided his riches. This son took his share and went to a distant land.

He wasted all his money on wicked living.
Soon he was hungry and had nothing to eat.
So he found a job feeding pigs.
He watched the pigs gobble down their food,
and he was so hungry he was willing to
share their meal.

Then the son remembered the good food his father fed the servants. He decided to go home. "I'll tell my father I'm sorry, and I'll ask him to forgive me," he thought.

"Maybe my father will hire me as a servant."

When the son returned home, his father ran
to him and kissed him.

The father said, "My son, you've come home!
I thought you were dead, but you're alive!"

Then the father had a great party for the lost
son who came home.

Jesus said to His followers, "This is how
God loves the sinner who is sorry."

LAZARUS LIVES!

"Jesus said to her, 'I am the resurrection and the life. He who believes in me will have life even if he dies. And he who lives and believes in me will never die.'" JOHN 11:25, 26

Jesus often stayed at the home of Mary, Martha, and Lazarus. Jesus enjoyed visiting with His friends. Sometimes Mary was so interested in what Jesus was saying that she forgot to do her chores.

But Martha spent her time cooking and
cleaning. Once Martha got upset and said,
"Lord, don't You care that I'm doing the work
alone? Please tell my sister to help me!"
Jesus said, "Mary is doing the most
important thing. She is listening to Me."

One day the sisters sent a message to Jesus:
"Lazarus is very sick!"
Jesus said to His followers, "This sickness
is so people can see the power of God and
praise Him."
Jesus loved Lazarus, but it was two days
before He went to see His friend.

When Jesus got there, Lazarus had died and
was buried in a cave.

Martha said, "Lord, if You had been here, my
brother wouldn't have died!"

Jesus replied, "He who believes in Me will
have life even if he dies." Mary fell at Jesus'
feet and cried. Jesus felt very sad.

Jesus prayed. Then He said, "Lazarus, come out!" Lazarus walked out of the cave. He was alive again!

Many people saw Jesus raise Lazarus from the dead. From then on, they believed in Jesus.

JESUS BLESSES THE CHILDREN

"Jesus said, 'Let the little children come to me. Don't stop them, because the kingdom of heaven belongs to people who are like these children.'" MATTHEW 19:14

One day Jesus' followers asked Him,
"Who is greatest in the kingdom of heaven?"
Jesus called a small child to His side.
He said, "The one who obeys and trusts Me
like this child is greatest in the Kingdom."

Jesus told His followers, "Children are very
important to God." Then Jesus told a story
to show how much God loves His children.
"A man had one hundred sheep. One sheep
got lost. The man left the other ninety-nine
sheep to search for the lost one."

"He searched everywhere until he found the lost sheep. The man was very happy. He put the sheep on his shoulders and carried it home. In the same way, your heavenly Father does not want any of His children to be lost."

Later, the people brought their children to Jesus so He could pray for them.
Jesus' followers thought He was too busy teaching to bother with babies. But Jesus said, "Let the children come to Me!"
He held the children and blessed them.

TEN HEALING MIRACLES

"When one of them saw that he was healed, he went back to Jesus. He praised God in a loud voice. Then he bowed down at Jesus' feet and thanked him." LUKE 17:15, 16

On the way to Jerusalem, Jesus met ten men. Their bodies were covered with ugly sores, and they were very sad.
They had left their families and friends so others would not catch their disease.

"Master, please help us!" they called.
Jesus said, "Go and show the priests that you are healed."
As the men obeyed Jesus, their sores went away.
All the men were happy they were healed.

One man hurried back to thank Jesus.
He said, "Glory to God, I'm healed!"
"Ten men were healed," said Jesus.
"Where are the other nine?"
Jesus was disappointed that they forgot to
praise God for their healing.
But He was pleased with the thankful man.

MARY ANOINTS JESUS

"Jesus answered, 'Let her alone. It was right for her to save this perfume for today—the day for me to be prepared for burial.'" JOHN 12:7

Jesus returned to Lazarus's house. Lazarus, Mary, and Martha held a dinner to honor Jesus. Martha served the food.
Lazarus ate with Jesus.
And Mary did something special to show Jesus how much she loved Him.

She poured a jar of costly perfume on Jesus'
head and feet. Then she wiped His feet with
her hair.

The smell of sweet perfume filled the room.
Jesus' followers said Mary was foolish to
waste the expensive perfume.

But Jesus was pleased with Mary's gift.

HOSANNA TO THE KING!

"They took branches of palm trees and went out to meet Jesus. They shouted, 'Praise God! God bless the One who comes in the name of the Lord! God bless the King of Israel!'" JOHN 12:13

Jesus stopped outside Jerusalem. He told His followers, "In the next town, you will find a donkey that has never been ridden. Untie the donkey and bring it to Me. Tell anyone who asks that it's for the Master."

The men brought the donkey to Jesus.
Then they laid their coats on the donkey's
back for Jesus to sit on.
Jerusalem was crowded with people for the
Passover Feast. Everyone was filled with
excitement!

A great crowd went out to meet Jesus as He
entered the city of Jerusalem.
The people shouted praises to God for
sending Jesus, the promised King.
They called, "Hosanna! Blessed is the King!"
They waved branches from palm trees and
spread their coats on the road like a carpet.

Loud praises filled the city.
But some of the Jewish leaders did not
believe in Jesus. They said, "Teacher, tell
Your followers to be quiet."
But Jesus said, "If the people don't praise Me,
even the rocks will cry out with joy!"

JESUS IN THE TEMPLE

"They asked Jesus, 'Do you hear the things these children are saying?' Jesus answered, 'Yes. Haven't you read in the Scriptures, "You have taught children and babies to sing praises"?'" MATTHEW *21:16*

The next morning, Jesus went into the temple. He was very upset by what He saw.
The temple workers were cheating the people. They were making the people pay a high price to worship at the temple. And the workers were keeping the money for themselves.

Jesus threw out all the greedy people
who were selling things in the temple.
He said, "It says in Scripture, 'My temple
will be called a house of prayer.'
But you have changed God's house
into a place for thieves!"

Then Jesus taught in the temple. He healed
blind and crippled people there.
The children sang praises to Him:
"Hosanna to the Son of David!"
This made the Jewish priests very angry.
They began making a plan to kill Jesus.

THE WIDOW'S GIFT

" 'She gave all she had.' " MARK 12:44

Jesus stood in the temple. He watched
the people bring their offerings to God.
The rich people smiled proudly. They put
large gifts of money in the offering box.

One poor woman dropped two small coins in the box. Jesus told His followers, "This poor widow gave more than the rest. Everyone else has plenty. They gave a little of what they did not need. She needed that money. But she gave all she had."

THE MASTER SERVES HIS FOLLOWERS

" 'I did this as an example for you. So you should do as I have done for you. I tell you the truth. A servant is not greater than his master.' "
JOHN *13:15, 16*

Jesus' followers asked Him, "Where do You want to eat the Passover feast?"
Jesus said, "Go into the city. You will find a man carrying a jar of water to a house. Tell the man the Teacher wants to use his house."

Everything happened as Jesus had said.
That evening Jesus and His twelve followers
went to the house. They ate their supper in
the large room upstairs. During the meal,
Jesus poured water into a bowl. Then He
began to wash the followers' feet.

Peter said, "Master, You shouldn't act like a
servant. I don't want You to wash my feet!"
But Jesus said, "If I don't wash you,
you can't be one of My people."
Peter cried, "Lord, please wash my hands
and head, too!"
Jesus taught them how to humbly serve others.

THE LAST MEAL

" 'I give you a new command: Love each other. You must love each other as I have loved you.' " JOHN 13:34

After Jesus washed His followers' feet,
He sat down with them.
Jesus knew it was almost time for Him
to go back to heaven.
He said, "One of you will turn against Me."

The followers were upset.
John asked, "Who will turn against You?"
Jesus dipped a piece of bread into the dish.
He said, "I will give this bread to the wicked
one." Jesus gave the bread to Judas.
Judas quickly left the room.

Jesus knew He would die for the sins of the people. He picked up the bread. He blessed it and broke it.

Then He gave it to the followers to eat. He said, "This bread is My body, given for you. Do this to remember Me."

After they ate, Jesus took the cup.
He thanked God for it.
He said, "This cup is a sign of the new
promise between God and His people.
Drink this. And remember My blood
will cover your sins."

Jesus said, "I will be leaving soon."
The followers felt very sad.
But Jesus cheered them up, "Don't worry.
My Father will give you another Helper.
He will send the Holy Spirit.
And later I will come back to you."

THE JUDAS KISS

"'Father, if it is what you want, then let me not have this cup of suffering. But do what you want, not what I want.'" LUKE *22:42*

When the meal was over, Jesus and His followers sang a song.
Then they went to a place to pray.
Jesus warned them, "Tonight you will all leave Me."

"I won't!" said Peter.
Jesus said, "Before morning, you will say
three times that you don't know Me."
Jesus was sad. He told Peter, James, and John,
"Stay awake and pray for strength."
Then Jesus knelt to pray.
An angel from heaven came to comfort Him.

When Jesus finished praying,
His followers were asleep.
"Wake up!" Jesus said. "The time has come!"
Just then, Judas led an angry crowd to Jesus.
They were carrying torches, swords, and clubs.

Judas promised to give Jesus to the Jewish
leaders for thirty pieces of silver. He acted like
a friend and kissed Jesus. That was how
Judas pointed out Jesus to the soldiers.

PETER'S LIE

". . . Jesus had told him: Before the rooster crows you will say . . . you don't know me.'" MATTHEW 26:75

The soldiers grabbed Jesus to arrest Him. Peter took a knife and cut off a man's ear. But Jesus cried, "Stop!" Then He touched the man's ear and healed him.

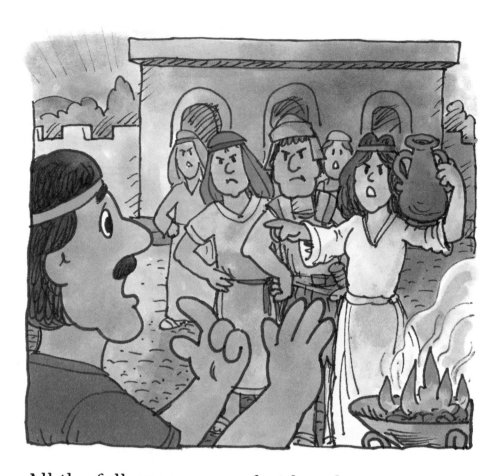

All the followers were afraid and ran away.
The soldiers took Jesus to the house of the
high priest. Peter followed far behind them.
In the courtyard, a servant girl asked Peter,
"Are you a follower of Jesus?"
Peter said, "No!"

Someone else said, "You were with Jesus!"
Again Peter said, "No, I wasn't!"
Later some people said, "You talk like Jesus."
Peter swore, "I don't know Him."
A rooster crowed, and Peter remembered
Jesus' words. Peter was very sorry.

THE LAMB OF GOD

"But Jesus said nothing. Again the high priest said to Jesus, 'You must swear to this. I command you by the power of the living God to tell us the truth. Tell us, are you the Christ . . . ?'" MATTHEW *26:63*

The lawyers told people to lie about Jesus to the Jewish court. When these people lied, Jesus said nothing.
Then the priest asked, "Are You God's Son?" Jesus said, "I am."

His answer made the people angry.
They spit on Him and slapped His face.
Then the Jewish leaders took Jesus before
Pilate, the Roman governor.
They told Pilate, "He claims to be a king!"

Pilate asked Jesus, "Are You a king?"
Jesus answered, "Yes. My kingdom is in
heaven." Pilate found nothing wrong with
Jesus. Pilate told the people that he was
going to release Jesus.

But the angry people yelled, "Kill Him!
Kill Him on a cross! Free the prisoner
Barabbas instead."
Pilate listened to the people.
He let Barabbas, the murderer, go free.
And he said Jesus must die on a cross.

THE CROSS

"Jesus cried out in a loud voice, 'Father, I give you my life.' After Jesus said this, he died." LUKE 23:46

The Roman soldiers beat Jesus. They dressed Him like a king to make fun of Him. Then they made Him carry a cross through the city.

The cross was very heavy. So the soldiers forced
a man in the crowd to help Jesus carry it.
Finally, they came to a place called Golgotha.
There, the soldiers nailed Jesus' hands and
feet to the cross.

Two criminals were nailed on crosses next
to Jesus. Jesus' followers were sad and cried.
But many people laughed at Him.
Jesus said, "Father, forgive them.
They don't know what they are doing."

When Jesus died, the sky turned black and
the earth shook. The soldiers were afraid.
They said, "He really *was* the Son of God!"
Jesus' body was laid in a tomb.
A large stone was rolled across the entrance
to the tomb.

HE'S ALIVE!

" 'Go quickly and tell his followers. Say to them: 'Jesus has risen from death.' " MATTHEW 28:7

On Sunday morning, Mary Magdalene
and some other women went to the tomb.
Just then there was an earthquake.
An angel came down from heaven and rolled
away the stone from the tomb.

The angel sat on the stone.
The soldiers guarding the tomb shook
with fear and became like dead men.
The angel told the women, "Don't be afraid. I
know you are looking for Jesus. But He is not
here. He is risen, as He said He would."

Then the angel said, "Go quickly. Tell
His followers Jesus has risen from death!"
The women hurried away. They were afraid
but happy. They ran to tell Jesus' followers
what had happened.

Suddenly Jesus stood before them.
The women fell down at His feet and
worshiped Him.
"Don't be afraid," Jesus said. "Tell My brothers
to go to Galilee. They will see Me there."

A MEALTIME MIRACLE

"While the two followers were telling this, Jesus himself stood among those gathered. He said to them, 'Peace be with you.'" LUKE 24:36

Jesus appeared to Peter, alone.
Then Peter told the followers,
"The Lord has really risen!" Later, eleven of
Jesus' followers were eating together.
Suddenly Jesus appeared to them, too.

The followers were very afraid.
They thought they were seeing a ghost.
But Jesus said, "Why do you doubt?
It is I Myself! See My hands and feet?"
They saw the scars on His hands and feet,
and they believed.

The followers were amazed and happy.
Jesus asked, "Do you have any food here?"
They gave Jesus some cooked fish to eat.
Jesus told them, "The Scripture says
the Messiah would be killed and would rise
from death on the third day."

Jesus said, "You have seen these things happen, just as the prophets said they would. Now go into all the world and tell the Good News. Tell people their sins will be forgiven when they turn to Me."

JESUS GOES HOME

" 'You saw Jesus taken away from you into heaven. He will come back in the same way you saw him go.' " ACTS 1:11

Jesus led His followers to a mountain outside the city.

He said, "In a few days, you will be baptized in the Holy Spirit. Don't leave Jerusalem until you receive this promise."

He said, "The Holy Spirit will give you power
to be My witnesses in all the world."
Jesus blessed them.
The followers worshiped Jesus.
Then He went up into the sky.

They watched Jesus being carried into heaven in a cloud. Suddenly two angels appeared. They said, "Jesus will come again in the same way you saw Him go!"

TONGUES OF FIRE

"Joel the prophet wrote . . . 'God says: I will give my Spirit freely to all kinds of people.'" ACTS 2:16–17

Each day Jesus' followers met together to pray. The believers were waiting for their promise from God.

During this time, the believers gathered
to celebrate Pentecost.
This was the Jewish Harvest Festival.
Suddenly a noise came from heaven.
It sounded like a strong wind blowing,
and it filled the whole house.

It looked like a tongue of fire
rested on the head of each believer.
The believers were all filled with the Holy
Spirit, and they began to speak in different
languages!

PEOPLE OF POWER

"'The Holy Spirit will come to you. Then you will receive power. You will be my witnesses.'" ACTS 1:8

Jewish people from every country were in Jerusalem for Pentecost.
They were surprised.
"How can this be?" they said. "We hear these believers speaking in our own languages about the great things God has done!"

Peter stood up and boldly told the people the good news about Jesus. "Be baptized in the name of Jesus Christ," Peter said. "Let Jesus forgive you and save you from sin! Then you will receive the Holy Spirit, too!"

The people who believed what Peter said
were baptized.
About 3,000 people were added to the
number of believers that day.

The believers spent much of their time together. They worshiped God in the temple each day. They also met in their homes to break bread and pray. They gave to the poor. And God blessed them with more new believers.

As the believers shared with each other, their
hearts were filled with joy. They praised God,
and God gave them everything they needed.
With great power, these followers
told people about Jesus.

A CRIPPLED MAN IS HEALED

"'By the power of Jesus Christ from Nazareth—stand up and walk!'"
ACTS 3:6

The followers did many miracles. One day,
Peter and John went to the temple to pray.
At the temple gate sat a crippled beggar.
The man asked Peter and John for money.

Peter said, "I don't have any money. But I
can give you something else. By the power
of Jesus—stand up and walk!"
The man jumped up.
He walked into the temple praising God.
The people were amazed.
Peter and John began preaching to them.

CAN'T STOP TALKING

"We cannot keep quiet. We must speak about what we have seen and heard." Acts 4:20

When the Jewish leaders heard that the crippled man could walk, they were very upset.
They asked Peter and John, "By what power did you do this miracle?"
Peter and John told them about Jesus.

The Jewish leaders saw that
Peter and John were not afraid.
The leaders knew then that these two men
had been with Jesus.
So they warned Peter and John not to teach
about Jesus anymore.

Peter and John said bravely,
"We can't stop talking about Jesus!
We won't stop praising His name!"
These two men had received power
from the Holy Spirit. And they would never
be the same.

SIGNS AND WONDERS

"'Help us to be brave by showing us your power; make sick people well, give proofs, and make miracles happen.'" Acts 4:30

The Jewish leaders tried to scare
the followers again. But the believers kept
speaking boldly in Jesus' name.
Crowds came to the city with their sick.
And all the people were healed.

The Jewish leaders were jealous.
They put Jesus' followers in jail.
But that night an angel opened the prison
doors. The next day the soldiers found Jesus'
followers preaching in the temple again.
The soldiers took them to the high priest.

The angry priest said, "We warned you not to talk about Jesus anymore!"
Peter said, "We must obey God, not men."
The Jewish leaders had Jesus' followers whipped. But the followers were glad to suffer for Jesus.

STEPHEN

"Stephen continued speaking: '. . . You have not given your hearts to God! You won't listen to him! You are always against what the Holy Spirit is trying to tell you.'" ACTS 7:51

Stephen helped the followers serve food to the poor people.
He was filled with the Holy Spirit.
God gave Stephen the power to do great miracles among the people.

The Jewish leaders were against Stephen.
They tried to argue with him.
But the Spirit gave him great wisdom.
And the Jewish leaders could not fight him.
So the leaders secretly paid some men to lie
about Stephen.

Many people believed the lies. Some of them grabbed Stephen and took him to the high priest.
The priest said, "Are these things true?"
Then Stephen began preaching about Jesus.
"Look!" Stephen pointed to the sky. "I see heaven open. Jesus is standing next to God!"

This made some of the Jewish leaders mad.
They took Stephen out of the city
and threw stones at him.
Stephen fell to his knees and cried,
"Lord, forgive them!"
And then he died.

Some of the Jewish leaders tried to
kill all the believers in Jerusalem.
Many people escaped from harm by
quickly moving to other cities.
These believers took the good news of Jesus
with them wherever they went.

THE MAGICIAN

"And everywhere they were scattered, they told people the Good News."
Acts 8:4

A believer named Philip went to Samaria to preach about Jesus. He healed the weak and crippled people there.

Many of the people had evil spirits in them. But Philip made the evil spirits go away.

In Samaria a magician named Simon
amazed people with his magic tricks.
His friends said he had "the Great Power."
Philip told Simon and his friends
about the power of Jesus.

They saw the miracles Philip did, and they
believed the good news of Jesus. Philip
baptized the new believers. Later, Peter and
John came to Samaria. They saw that the
new believers had not yet received the Holy
Spirit. Peter and John placed their hands on
the people and prayed for them.

The new believers received the Holy Spirit. When Simon saw this, he offered Peter money for this power. Peter said, "You're full of jealousy and sin! You can't buy God's gift!" Simon said, "Please pray that the Lord will forgive me." So Peter and John prayed for Simon.

PHILIP BAPTIZES A RICH MAN

"Both Philip and the officer went down into the water, and Philip baptized him." Acts 8:38

An angel told Philip to go to the desert road that leads to Gaza from Jerusalem.
On the road, Philip saw an important officer from Ethiopia.
The man was sitting in his chariot, reading Scripture.

The Spirit told Philip, "Go to the chariot!"
So Philip ran up to the side of the chariot.
And he asked the man, "Do you understand
what you are reading?"
The man said, "I need someone to explain
it to me!"
Philip gladly explained God's Word, and
told the man about Jesus.
The man believed and was baptized.

SAUL SEES THE LIGHT

"The Lord Jesus sent me. He is the one you saw on the road on your way here." ACTS 9:17

In Jerusalem, a Jewish leader called Saul tried to frighten the followers of Jesus. Saul went from house to house, searching for believers.
When he found followers of Jesus, he threw them in jail.

One day Saul was on his way to the city of Damascus. He was going there to look for believers, too.

Suddenly a bright light from heaven blinded him. He fell to the ground.

A voice from heaven said, "Saul, why are you doing things against Me?"

Saul asked, "Who are You, Lord?"
"I am Jesus!" the voice answered. "I am the
One you are trying to hurt!"
Then Jesus told Saul to go to Damascus
and wait for someone to help him. Saul
opened his eyes, but he could not see!

The men traveling with Saul heard the voice,
too. But they saw no one!
The men took Saul by the hand and led
him into the city. For three days, Saul could
not see, and he did not drink or eat.

Ananias, a follower of Jesus, lived in
Damascus. The Lord spoke to Ananias in a
vision. "Quickly, go to Straight Street. Find
the house of Judas. Ask for Saul. Tell him
about Me!"

Ananias was afraid because he had heard
that Saul hated all believers.

Still, Ananias obeyed the Lord. He found Saul
praying in the house of Judas. He put
his hands on Saul's eyes. Ananias said,
"Saul, the Lord Jesus sent me to you. Jesus
wants you to see again and be filled with the
Holy Spirit!" At once Saul could see!

PAUL IN A BASKET

"Soon he began to preach about Jesus in the synagogues, saying, 'Jesus is the Son of God!'" ACTS 9:20

Saul was happy to learn the truth about Jesus. Now he knew Jesus really was the promised Son of God!
And he began telling other people about the Good News.

Saul became known as Paul, the preacher.
He was a changed man!
The Jewish leaders planned to kill Paul.
But some followers helped Paul escape
by lowering him over the city wall in a
basket.

RISE AND BE HEALED!

". . . He turned to the body and said, 'Tabitha, stand up!' She opened her eyes, and . . . sat up." ACTS 9:40

Peter preached in Joppa.
A woman named Tabitha lived there.
She always helped the poor.
And the people loved her dearly.
Suddenly Tabitha became sick and died.
The believers quickly sent for Peter.

When Peter got there, some poor widows
were standing around the dead body
crying.
"Look at our beautiful clothes," the women
cried. "Tabitha made them for us."
Then Peter told everyone to leave the room.
He prayed for Tabitha. She opened her eyes
and sat up!

THE HOLY SPIRIT IS FOR EVERYONE

"God accepts anyone who worships him and does what is right. It is not important what country a person comes from." ACTS 10:35

A soldier named Cornelius loved God. He prayed daily and gave money to poor people. One day he saw a vision. An angel said, "God is pleased with your gifts. He hears your prayers. I will bring Peter to your house, and he will preach to you."

Peter also had a strange vision.
In it the Holy Spirit told him to eat things
forbidden by Jewish law! Then the Spirit told
him that some men were looking for him.
The Spirit said, "Go with these men to their
house. Preach to them. I have sent them."

Peter obeyed the Holy Spirit.
He went with the men. He told Cornelius
and his family about Jesus. While they were
listening, the Holy Spirit came into their
hearts. They began speaking in languages
they had not learned! Peter was amazed.

Now Peter understood his vision.
The Holy Spirit is for people from every
country. The good news of Jesus is not just
for Jewish people! Peter baptized the new
believers. Then he ate with his new friends.

A MISSION

"They laid their hands on Barnabas and Saul and sent them out."
ACTS 13:3

One day Paul was worshiping the Lord with a group of believers. Some of these people were prophets. The Holy Spirit said to them, "I have chosen Paul and the believer Barnabas to do a special job."

The people prayed. They placed their hands on Paul and Barnabas. The believers blessed them.

Then they sent Paul and Barnabas to preach the Good News in other lands.

LIGHT AND DARKNESS

"He looked straight at Elymas and said, '. . . You are full of evil tricks. . . . You are always trying to change the Lord's truth into lies! Now the Lord will touch you, and you will be blind.'" ACTS 13:9–11

In Paphos, the governor wanted to hear the message of God. Paul and Barnabas preached to him.

But a false prophet named Elymas didn't want the governor to hear God's Word.

Elymas tried to keep the governor from
believing in Jesus. Paul told Elymas,
"The Lord will make you blind for trying to
change His truth into lies!"
Suddenly Elymas could not see.
The governor saw this miracle and believed.

THE FORTUNE-TELLER

" 'These men are servants of the Most High God! They are telling you how you can be saved!' " ACTS 16:17

One day Paul and his friend Silas were going to a prayer meeting near the river.
They met a slave girl who had an evil spirit.
She began to shout at them.
She wouldn't keep quiet.

The girl was a fortune-teller. She told people
what was going to happen to them. She
made lots of money for her owners. For
many days she followed Paul and Silas.
Again and again she shouted, "These men
are servants of the Most High God!"

Finally Paul said, "By the power of
Jesus Christ, I tell you to come out of her!"
At once, the evil spirit came out of the girl.
She became calm and quiet.
But her owners were very angry. They
couldn't use her to make money anymore.

PRAISES FROM PRISON

". . . 'Believe in the Lord Jesus and you will be saved—you and all the people in your house.'" ACTS 16:31

Paul and Silas were beaten and
thrown into prison.
About midnight, they were praying
and singing songs to God.
The other prisoners were listening to them.

Suddenly an earthquake shook the jail.
The doors of the prison broke open.
The prisoners' chains fell off!
The jail guard woke up with a jolt.
He thought all his prisoners had escaped.
The jailer was very upset. He reached for
his sword to kill himself.

Paul shouted, "Don't worry! We're here."
The jailer shook with fear and fell down
before Paul and Silas.
"What must I do to be saved?" he asked.
They said, "Believe in the Lord Jesus.
Then you and your family will be saved!"

The jailer took Paul and Silas home with
him. He washed their wounds and gave them
food to eat. Then Paul and Silas told the
jailer and his family about Jesus.
The jailer's family was baptized.
They were filled with joy!

PAUL IS ARRESTED

"I have fought the good fight. I have finished the race. I have kept the faith." 2 Timothy 4:7

Paul preached about Jesus all his life.
When Paul grew old, he was arrested again
for being a follower of Jesus.
Soldiers took Paul to Rome in chains.
He spent the rest of his life in jail. But even in
prison, he preached about Jesus.

LETTERS FROM PRISON

"I can do all things through Christ because he gives me strength."
PHILIPPIANS *4:13*

Paul wrote many letters to cheer up
the believers he had met in his travels. In the
letters he told his friends, "Give thanks
whatever happens. Do not stop the work of
the Holy Spirit!"

"Learn the Word of God," Paul's letters said.
"Pray in the Spirit at all times.
Remember to keep the faith.
And never give up!"

THE CITY OF GOD

"Hallelujah! Our Lord God rules. He is the All-Powerful."
Revelation 19:6

One day John was worshiping God.
 He heard a loud voice that said,
"I am the start and the finish!"
Jesus appeared, dressed in a white robe.
 He was shining like a bright light.
John fell at His feet in fear.

Jesus said, "Do not be afraid. I am going to show you things no man has ever seen. Write these things in a book, and send it to the churches." The power of the Spirit carried John to a high mountain. He saw the golden city of heaven. All the people who love Jesus live there forever with God.

There is no crying or dying in the city of God.
There is no more sickness or sadness.
The Devil will be destroyed forever.
Everyone there is singing and serving God.
The city does not need sunshine. God's
glory is bright enough light for everyone to see.

Then John saw God's throne.
A rainbow was over the throne.
A beautiful river that looked like glass lay
before it. Next to God's throne were angels
saying, "Holy, holy, holy is the Lord."
Many people were worshiping at God's feet.

CHRIST'S RETURN

"'Listen! I am coming soon! He who obeys the words of prophecy in this book will be happy.'" REVELATION *22:7*

The sky opened. And John saw Jesus sitting on a white horse.

Jesus said, "I am coming to take My children to heaven with Me. I will punish people who do not love Me. I will bless the people who obey Me. Be ready, for I am coming soon!"